AF472498

# A Simple Guide for the Clueless, on Using the Internet to Build and Protect Your Investments.

By Richard I. Overall Sr.

Featuring Option Trading Basics

*This book is a work of non-fiction. Unless otherwise noted, the author and the publisher make no explicit guarantees as to the accuracy of the information contained in this book and in some cases, names of people and places have been altered to protect their privacy.*



*ISBN: 1-4107-9660-4 (e)*
*ISBN: 1-4107-9659-0 (sc)*

*Printed in the United States of America*
*Bloomington, IN*

*This book is printed on acid free paper.*

*Unless otherwise indicated, all scripture quotations are from the KING JAMES VERSION.*

1st Books - rev. *3/28/2006*

# Table of Contents

# Disclaimers

1 Akamai. The information provided about future expectations, plans and prospects of all the stocks mentioned in this book constitute forward-looking statements for purposes of the safe harbor provisions under The Private Securities Litigation Reform Act of 1995. Actual results may differ materially from those indicated by these forward-looking statements as a result of various important factors including, but not limited to, the dependence on service and technology products, the effects of any attempts to intentionally disrupt our services or network by hackers or others, failure of our telecommunications suppliers to provide sufficient transmission capacity, a failure of Akamai's network infrastructure, and 's Annual Report on Form 10-K, quarterly reports on Form 10-Q, and other documents periodically filed with the SEC.

2 Calypte biomedical, Proxity, Janus worldwide, Silicon Graphic, Microsoft and Electric city.

Statements in this book that are not historical facts are forward-looking statements within the meaning of the Securities Act of 1933, as amended. Those statements include statements regarding the intent, belief or current expectations of the Companies and its management. Such statements reflect management's current views, are based on certain assumptions and involve risks and uncertainties. Actual results, events, or performance may differ materially from the above forward-looking statements due to a number of important factors, and will be dependent upon a variety of factors, including, but not limited to, our ability to obtain additional financing and access funds from our existing financing arrangements that will allow us to continue our current and future operations and whether demand for our product and testing service in domestic and international markets will continue and expand. The Companies undertakes no obligation to publicly update these forward-looking statements to reflect events or circumstances that occur after the date hereof or to reflect any change in the Companies expectations with regard to these forward-looking statements or the occurrence of unanticipated events. Factors that may impact the Companies success are more fully disclosed in the Companies most recent public filings with the U.S. Securities and Exchange Commission ("SEC"), including its annual report on Form 10-K/A (No.1) for the year ended December 31, 2001 and its subsequent filings with the SEC.

3. Disclaimer: It is not the intention of the author to promote the sale of any of the stocks or mutual funds in this book. The stocks chosen are simply examples used to promote how the Internet can help you with your investment needs.

# Acknowledgements

When I began this book I had little idea as to how it would turn out. But God as usual made provision by the way of people who would help me translate my thoughts into sensible reading. I like to thank my Pastor and his wife for their support.

Mr. Peter Daniels of Australia who's visit to Word of Faith Christian Center Southfield brought great inspiration to my life as well as many other's.

I thank God for the tireless efforts of Daniel Livingston, Renella Thomas, Margareta Overall and for their patience in proofreading this book. I know it was like translating Chinese into English. Special thanks to my prayer partners and friends.

# Dedication

To my daughter Piquette

# Introduction

When I talk to people about investing, they seem to know all the negative events that have happened over the years. Some even remark about the great stock market fall in 1929. Strangely though, they don't know that there were some people, like John D. Rockefeller and J.P. Morgan who made a fortune during that same period because at the proper time they sold their stock. Warren Buffett who is presently the second richest man in the world, made his entire fortune as an investor. Like Rockefeller and Morgan he followed simple basic principles such as watching their investments and investing in companies with good fundamentals.

Neither of them had the Internet. Today the Internet has made it easy for anyone to become a savvy investor. Most investors thought that mutual funds and CD's were the ultimate safe investments until March 2000. Then the stock market went down.

A lot of investors saw their portfolio dive with the market. One thing that most people did was to leave their investments completely in the hands of their financial advisor. They found out, that their advisor wasn't paying any attention to their money. If you called them they probably told you to stay in for the long haul instead of taking the profits and repurchasing your stock or mutual fund at a lower price with the profits. I doubt that they would risk guaranteeing paying your losses, if your portfolio doesn't go back up in value. How can your one broker keep up with a thousand accounts on a day to day basis? Well hopefully you will read this book and find the courage to pick up the pieces and get back the money you loss.

The best way to get over your fear of handling your own investments, is to learn how the Stock Market works. It is a lot easier now with the help of the Internet.

If you have a 401k, 403b, **SEP (S**implified **E**mployee **P**ension plan), **ESOP** (**E**mployee **S**tock **O**ption **P**lan.) or **I.R.A.** (**I**ndividual **R**etirement **A**ccount) you can accept the status quo and do nothing. You can choose not to retire, or live at a much lower standard after you retire. You can also take this opportunity to maximize your benefit, by learning to use the Internet and develop your investments.

You must to understand that the days of employers looking out for your retirement are gone forever. The older retirement plans were called **Defined Benefit.** The company would pay a premium to a Investment service and the company had the responsibility of making sure there would be enough money in the retirement plan **regardless** of the stock market condition. If the money weren't there, they would have to pay it out of their profits, unless they filed bankruptcy and the Bankruptcy court would let them out of paying the retirement. By 2004 over 3200 companies eliminated pensions through bankruptcies and the numbers keep climbing.

Large companies like General Motors is regularly complaining about pension and health care cost.

Nowadays you have what are called **Defined Contribution** plans. **You**, not your employer, has the responsibility to make sure that you have enough money to retire. Without the knowledge of how your particular plan works, you could very well end up retiring with a reduced living standard or unable to retire at all.

I believe that the reasons that employers switched to the newer type of plans are:

1. They don't have to pay for losses when the stock market goes down.

2. They are cheaper for them to maintain.

3. Like Social Security there will be fewer people paying into the fund which would cost them more under the old system.

4. Future cost like pensions and medical benefits eat up profits.

Something else I want to point out is, the money you make from selling stock comes from the company. This is listed on the Financial report as **Distributions and it is considered a liability ( loss).** Even though your investment in them, pay's for development, product research, service improvement, expansion, and operating cost, if enough of a stock is sold at a certain time the stock price could fall and the company could suffer. This is one reason brokers don't call you and tell you to sell. It hurts the profit picture. Which also will bring the stock price down.

Some times a company official sells his stock, because he is aware of some internal problems that may be forth coming. It used to be approximately [1]30 days before you find out and your investment could be lost. The reason I say could be lost, is because there is a way to protect your investment. Which is one reason I wrote this book. As an F.Y.I. company officers have to report stock sales within 48 hrs. Per the sarbanes/oxley law.

A broker isn't required to automatically call you and tell you to sell. But you can program your computer to do it. He isn't by law required to look out for your best interest.

Look what happened to some of the people at Enron who could sell their stock but didn't. I heard one man say on TV before a Senate committee he thought his "broker" would take care of him. He lost over a million dollars from his entire retirement. He had worked for 30 years to build it. Why didn't his broker help him?

The Internet and television has brought investing ability for the average individual to a new level. The ability to research and monitor your investments has become much easier. I'm not going to tell you everything about Internet investing, because I don't know everything. I will be covering some basic things that other professionals over- looked. I believe this book will help you realize that you can be wealthy or at the very least retire at a comfortable level. You can continue to improve, increase and protect your investment long after you retire, and avoid unnecessary losses.

Hopefully you will exchange some of your soap opera or comedy hour time for some stock market research time. If you have children that will be attending college in the next 10 years you can learn about companies that cost .15 cents a share like Microsoft did when it started in 1986. It rose to $120.00 a share in December 1999. A $1500.00 investment would have made $1,200,000.00. Did you get the same return from your 401k? Would that help pay college tuition?

With some effort and time you will become secure and skillful in investing in your future and that of your children. Also you will obtain a skill that you can pass on to your children and use after retirement. I can only stress that pro-active involvement from you will make the difference between your having to substitute dog food for meat with your meals or being able to eat healthy when you retire. Remember that the cost of living isn't going to go down just because you retired.

[1] This has been changed to 48 hrs.

My primary reason for writing this book, is solely to let the average person know that the Internet can help them build and protect their investments. Now you can see information, that not long ago, was for brokers, analyst and the rich, and it is easy to understand.

The information in this book is only a small portion of the vast information that is available. Take advantage of it.

Godspeed in your quest.

Richard I Overall Sr.

# Learning the Language of the Stock Market

Let's get right down to business. First let's start with the TV and the Internet. If you feel fearful or are just uninformed about the Internet get your teenager (smile) or your neighbor's teenager to help you.

If you don't have a computer, go to local library. These days, Gateway or Dell are selling them for about $600.00. Call the Video Professor 1-800-309-1376 for a free disk on using the Internet. ($6.95 for shipping and handling). If you can afford it I recommend using cable Internet. The speed will be of great benefit. Start watching **CNBC** or **Bloomberg** financial TV news network. Stock market language is essential for everyone today. They transmit by their language which way the market going. When you see several analyst from different brokerages saying something like" We expect a market correction, which means it is going to go down pay attention. They control the stock market. If they say it still have some upside, follow their lead.

You don't have to watch it all day. If you can't get home in time, set your VCR to tape it at least for 1 hour, preferably 2 hours. Listen, soap operas and the History channel are all right, but they won't help you prepare for retirement, start a business debt free, or buy a yacht with cash. Once you have gotten familiar with what is going on you will have time to get back to whatever entertainment you like. You will have the comfort of knowing that your money is working for you instead of against you.

On CNBC, The writing that goes across the bottom of the screen on is called a **ticker**. It provides what is called Real-Time information. It let's you know some of the major trading activity. This service used to be reserved for the wealthy. No one else could afford it unless they were already a millionaire. I learned at a seminar that it probably would cost you $100,000.00 a year to have access to it. You had to pay the NASDAQ and NYSE for access. Then you had to pay the Phone Company for connection at about 1.25 cents a minute from 9:30 a.m. to 4 p.m. A kind, generous person or company (May God Bless their every endeavor) pays for this.

Each day they tell you who the sponsor is. **USE THE TICKER to learn about stock momentum buys.** I will show you the reason why later when we get to the Charting section.

I'll explain what you're looking at. The top white line is the **NYSE** (New York Stock Exchange) and the bottom blue line is the **NASDAQ** (National Association of Stock Dealers and Automated Quotation system). Recently stocks that trade on the **AMEX** (American Stock Exchange) are shown on the blue line. AMEX stocks have 3 letters and NASDAQ stocks have 4 and sometimes 5. The fifth letter tells you something that is happening with the company. This information is found in the glossary at **NASDAQ.COM**. NYSE stocks usually have 2 or 3 letters. The company chooses the letters for its symbol.

So, generally what you see going across the screen is this**, SGI 100@ 1.30 ^ .25**. This reads "Company symbol" SGI (Silicon Graphics), someone bought 100 shares @= at $1.30 and the price since closing yesterday is up (in green w/ triangle pointing up .25 cents. If the triangle is pointing down and red, it is down .25 cents). Just for the record this is similar to how you read the stock listing in the newspaper. They don't show the shares purchased. They show the symbol, the price, the highest and lowest price it reached over the last 52 weeks. It may show some different information also. The 52-week high is the price it will hopefully return to. For some reason it has dipped below it. If something other than a recession caused to fall, you need to find out. Sometimes the stock is sold to bring the price down on purpose. This usually occurs when a downgrade is announced. This allows for the stock to be repurchased at a lower price and to make even more money as the stock goes back up in price. So if a stock is at it's 52 week high you may want to do the same thing they do. You must also watch to see if it will go to a new 52 week high. This could mean higher price, which means more profit.

In the charting section I will show you how to back track a stock's price history. You can check the news archives to see what caused the decline. If there was no bad news then it was probably just profit taking.

Your broker or financial advisor is not likely to call you and tell you to take some profits. You will have to avail yourself of this opportunity. You can put the money back to work in the same stock if you like when the decline stops. Again you will be able to tell by watching the charts.

In 1999 they began allowing the general public to trade for the first time before the market open at 8 a.m. and after hours which is after 4 P.M. Eastern Time until 7 p.m. Stock symbols that are traded after hours will appear in gold. These are mostly seasoned traders, and isn't recommended for beginners.

Not every online brokerage offer after hours trading. In the future trading will be 24 hours around the world on all the different exchanges. They are building the system for it now as you are reading this. This will allow money to be made 24 hours a day. That's another reason to learn this. They show the European market a 4 A.M. est. on CNBC. For professional traders this info gives them some idea where The American market might go that day

The NASDAQ trades at 8.A.M. in the morning. Pre-hour and after hour trades are done person to person via a **ECN** (Electronic Communication Network). This is a question you may want answered before you choose a Online Brokerage "Do they trade pre and after hours? You might not need it in the beginning, but I guarantee you will want to after you see how much money you can make doing this. This is also why I recommend taping **CNBC**. For traders (short term investors) this is a good place to shop for a good investment.

About momentum plays. You will have to be proficient in using charts to be able to buy in and get out at a profitable time. **This is not for amateurs**.

What frequently happens is that a stock will start shooting up in price. This move will usually be dramatic. A stock can go up in price 1 to 20 dollars. If you have the time to sit at the computer, this can translate into major fast money. Nowadays you can access the system via cellphone. Cellphones now feature internet access. This allows mobile trading. Treo or Blackberry would be best for this.

The NYSE and AMEX don't start trading until 9:30 A.M. After the trading starts, only certain stocks will travel across the screen. It's not possible to show every stock being traded. With certain online brokerage sites like Ameritrade, E-trade or Scottrade offer what is called a Streamer. The Streamer allows you to watch the moment to moment buying and selling of any particular stock. So it is possible to watch only the stocks you are interested in. The NASDAQ.COM, and CNBC.COM sites allow you to set up a ticker with specific stocks you choose. A stock screener can be used to locate stocks to invest in or trade. I will discuss that later.

On the right lower part of the screen, will be stats on how the Dow Jones Industrial Average, the NASDAQ, and S&P Index (Standard and Poor) is doing. This may indicate how that Market may go that day. If you go to this website **www.fool.com/Features/1996/sp0529a.htm** you will learn about a journalist named Charles Dow who created the Dow Jones average. It is simple reading and can help you understand more about it.

Basically the Dow Jones Average consist of **30** companies that are the believed to be the best performing at that time in their particular sector, such as Health care, Technology, Financial, Food service, Consumer goods etc. The NASDAQ covers about 5000. They also have the NASDAQ 100. The NASDAQ works by the same principle. They aren't the entire stock market. They are only a segment of the market.

However, the Dow and NASDAQ can be going down while a particular stock might be going up. They have great influence on the Market and are an excellent guide to be utilized, particularly for long term investments. They are not a tell all of where the entire stock market is as a whole. There is never a 100 % decline in the market. There are always stocks going up. Again a stock screener can locate them. In Oct.1999 to Jan. 2000 I was able to make 300% on one stock that I traded twice. During the same period, the DOW and the NASDAQ were going the opposite way, down. I was able to do this by understanding how charts operate.

Long term investors should pay attention to the DOW, particularly those with 401k's and similar type retirement plans. If it has climbed up several thousand points and starts a serious drop like it did in March 2000, then you need to look at moving your investment to the safe or guaranteed portion of your 401k. It should have one, if it doesn't sell it and get one that does.

Safe would be Guaranteed Fund like a Bond fund or Money market. Bonds generally go opposite of the stock market or equities as they are sometimes called.

There are two financial rating companies Standard and Poor and Moody's. They set the level of a company's credit worthiness. Standard and Poor, is also known as the **S&P as in S&P 500.** If they upgrade a company or downgrade a company you will see an almost immediate effect on the stock price. This may be a time to sell your stock and buy it back when price settles, if there are no serious internal problems with the company. Brokerage firms do upgrades and downgrades also and may have the same impact on the stock price.

In the **Research** section you will see how to get an inside view of what is going on financially at the company. However knowledge of downgrades will help you spot an opportunity to profit from a company for a cheaper price resulting in a higher gain in the future. Most downgrades of good companies are not permanent, and can be profitable.

Certain online brokerage's like Ameritrade give you access to Standard and Poor for a Stock evaluation. I have to say that S& P is pretty reliable. I noticed that during the Enron and Worldcom turmoil that they were not suspected of over rating Enron or Worldcom. I would consider their advice on buying, holding and selling. **Briefing.com** list companies that are upgraded and downgraded.

[2]**CNBC** is a world class and very informative news cast. I recommend that you watch **CNBC** daily. It will help you become familiar with investing business language. It's much better than the Local Blues News anyway. I would also suggest watching all the feature shows like Larry Kudlow and Co. who will keep you connected between Mainstreet, Wallstreet and Washington, Jim Cramer's Mad Money who will educate you why and whynot to buy certain com- panies. He also makes some excellent stock picks. You must watch Suze Orman on the weekend. Suze Orman focuses on helping you get your financial life together. You would have to pay to get what she is giving away. If you don't have money to invest you start watching her and you will have money to invest.

At any time of the day their will be someone on CNBC that will help you through this maze of investing.

[2] I don't get paid to mention CNBC.

# Research

Ok, Now to do a little stock research. This where you can research those stocks you might find on the **CNBC** ticker, **USA TODAY** business section, **NASDAQ.COM,OTCBB.COM, Yahoo stock screener, Investor Business daily 100** or in your **Prospectus.**When I started, I knew had a portfolio, but I really didn't know what a Portfolio was. So go to **WWW.FOOL.COM**. Now on the right, click on **Fool School**. Now click on **Financial Glossary**. Click on **P**. Slide the bar down. You should see the word **Portfolio**.

**Portfolio**: All the securities held by an individual, institution, or mutual fund.

Almost every financial term you need to know can be found here. Nearly every financial site you go to has a glossary. This is important because some of the words you hear on CNBC or read in the newspaper will be better understood when you have the definition.

Here's one **Prospectus**. Sound familiar? That's that book you get annually that you throw away because you can't understand it.

**Prospectus**: A legal document usually written in extraordinarily tedious language that provides information about a potential investment, including

discussions of its investment objectives, policies, past performance, risks, and cost. (Fool's translation).

Once you figure out your Prospectus, it can be used to find good low priced growth stocks to buy. The good part is that they have done most of the research for you. They picked the companies based on certain criteria. All you have to do is search through the prospectus for the stocks that will give you the growth that you want. The companies will be listed by names. All you have to do is get the symbol. You can do that by typing the name into the quote box. There is a easier way.

Don't get discouraged. No one was born knowing this stuff. The purpose of this book is to help you accomplish your financial goal without having to get a M.B.A from Harvard. The Harvard guys put this together, you just have to learn to use it. Believe me, they have done 80% of the work for you. If you look through it you will find many different companies listed. You will be able to go to the Internet and research them.

Another excellent website to learn definitions is **Investopedia .com**. At that site in the search box on the upper right, you can type in whatever word you need explained. The answer will appear in layman's terms.

Go to **WWW.MSN.COM**. Now click on **Money** on the left. For the purpose of research type in [3]**AKAM** (Akamai Technologies) in the box that say's **Quote** on the right. It was $4.57 when this was written.

This is the stock quote page. It has valuable information on it. On the left you is a list of hyperlinks. They reveal the financial state of the company.

It also comes equipped with a Research Wizard that will help you understand the information provided. Note the large number in the center with the square around it. That's a rating number. It goes from 1 to 10. Look for 4 or better. The higher the number the lower the risk. But usually when the number is higher than 5, the price is higher. I've found most stocks in the $ 2.00 range with good earnings, low debt and a 5 tend to grow in a 3 year

---

[3] See disclaimer

span of time, some times even less. It is possible to find stocks with a lower rating as low as 3 with growing revenue that could be profitable in the future. Study them carefully before you buy them. **Time is on your side**, don't rush. One of the keys to successful investing is patience.

One of the most important links is **Research Wizard.** Click it. It tell's you what to look for when you are considering investing in a company. As you click on the word **Next** on the right, it gives you more detailed information. This information will be useful when you go to **Financial Results.** Now click on **Financial Results.** Two important aspects here to look at: **Sales**, do they make money? **Debt Equity,** how much of the revenue do they have to spend on operating? Assets minus Liability. If the **D/E** is more than .90 it should be a company that has high volume of product sales like a food store or a gas station. If you find a company that has any digit on the left of the decimal I would watch the company but avoid buying it until the number on the left of the decimal disappears.

Sometimes when a company buy's another company, they increase their debt load. If they time it right, and don't run into unforseen disasters, they may return to profitability. Bottom line, the lower the debt, higher the revenue, the better. An exception maybe a new companies with a new product or service idea that have patent control. A company that will have **large impact on a large segment of society** like Sirius (SIRI) or XM satellite radio (XMSR). Their product will be offered in almost every vehicle made in the future for a long period of time. When Microsoft started they probably started out in debt. It depends on the company and what impact they might have on society. Remember that statement **"Impact on Society"**. Warren Buffet saw that

Gillette would have a impact on society (along with a strong balance sheet) with the invention of the disposable razor. Back then, a lot of men were still using straight razors for those of us who are old enough to know what those are.

Now click on **Key Ratios**. Now click **Financial Condition.** Observe **Current ratio and Quick Ratio.** Basically these terms tell you how well a company pay's it's bills and how well it's cash is flowing. The higher the numbers the better. Now go back to **Fool.com** and look up those terms.

**Current ratio**

The current ratio provides a speedy indication of a company's ability to meet short-term debt obligations. The higher the ratio, the more liquid the company is, and they are able it is to take care of any short-term

debt. To determine the ratio, take current assets and divide by current liabilities.

**Quick ratio**

Current assets minus inventories divided by current liabilities. By taking inventories out of the equation, you can check and see if a company has sufficient liquid assets to meet short-term operating needs. Are you getting the picture? Do you see how they have made the research easier? Before you had to call the company and write to the Security Exchange Com- mission to request this information. This took about 2 weeks. Then you had to sit down with a calculator and try to figure out all ratios, If you knew the formula.

## Earning per share

**Earnings Per Share (EPS).** Earnings, also known as net income or net profit, is the money that is left over after a company pays all of its bills. For many investors, earnings are the most important factor in analyzing a company. This where you try to figure out what the company will earn in the future. To allow for apples-to-apples comparisons, those who look at earnings use earnings per share (EPS).

You calculate the earnings per share by dividing the dollar amount of the earnings a company reports over the past 12 months by the number of shares it currently has outstanding. Thus, if XYZ Corp. has 1 million shares outstanding and has earned $1 million in the past 12 months, it has an EPS of $1.00.

$$\frac{\$1,000,000}{1,000,000 \text{ shares}} = \$1.00 \text{ in earnings per share (EPS)}$$

## P/E RATIO

**Price/Earnings Ratio (P/E).** Earnings per share alone mean absolutely nothing. In order to get a sense of how expensive or cheap a stock is, you have to look at those earnings relative to the stock price. To do this, most investors employ the price/earnings (P/E) ratio. The P/E ratio takes the stock price and divides it by the last four quarters' worth of earnings. If XYZ Corp. is currently trading at $25 a share with $1.00 of earnings per share (EPS), it would have a P/E of 25.

$25 share price
$1.00 in trailing EPS = 25 P/E

In the Key Ratio section, click on Price ratio to get this information. As you can see from the definition that it is essential to check this information out. But you can also see that it is easy to find out. Now at a glance you can know the financial health of a company. This is how growth potential is determined. Looking at the graph, each year should be improving.

Don't let this information frighten you. Remember how overwhelmed you were your first day on the job? Now you can do it with a blindfold. Spend some time on this site. It is one of the easiest to work with. Before you know it you will be wizzing through this. After you learn this site you may want to try Standard and Poors, Yahoo.com/finance,or Hoover.com. websites like Investor.com (Investor Business daily) and Vectorvest.com have done most of the homework for you, all you have to do is read the information. They charge a small annual fee that in my experience is well worth it.

Now go back to the left and click on **Insider Trading.** Insider trading shows you when company officers and major stockholders buy or sell their stock. Now click on **Recent Transaction**. It takes you back to see who is buying or selling stock. Buying is always a good sign. Selling can be bad if there are other issues.

One issue is the general Stock Market environment. Another could be internal problems within the company.

At the time of this writing it is November 2002. The Market has just gone through three years of turmoil. The tech bubble burst in March 2000, and then the chaotic Presidential Election, the China crisis, **911,** the hunt for Bin Laden. All of these events hurt earning reports, which shook investors confidence. Then the corporate fraud of Enron and Worldcom, a potential war with Iraq, and a nutty sniper running loose in the Washington D.C. area. Those events no doubt caused a lot of stock to be sold. But it also created the stock buying opportunities of a life time for those with investing knowledge and patience.

The March 2000 fall off is the real issue to focus on. The **charting** section is extremely important knowledge, and will show you how to protect your gains. You will see how a person could have sold their stock for profit in 2000, then waited by watching the charts, and know almost exactly when to put the money back in 2003.

Another reason an executive might engage in insider trading is to buy something personal like a new yacht or build a bigger home. You can know by watching the Charts to see if the stock price begins to decline beyond safety. The general rule is if stock drops 20% from it's maximum, you need to investigate why. If the stock charts are pointing downward continually, you should follow through with a sell. You should check your portfolio at least once a day. In a low profit environment like 2001-2002 their were a lot of bankruptcies. By observing up and down trends you can buy and sell the same stock over and over again. Each time you will be buying more and selling for a larger profit as time goes by.

Bottom line is that you can know through the Internet what is going on with your investments.

Now I want to examine something you might find familiar, a Mutual fund. [4] I've learned that the wealthy don't buy mutual funds. Your 401k is probably total mutual funds. For the purpose of this example I will use one that I once owned, Janus Worldwide. The symbol is JAWWX. If you need to find the symbol of one that you own (provided it has one, not all of them do). You just click **Find Symbol** type in the name of the stock or mutual fund and it should come up. You can always call the company to see if they have one, or they will tell you which Index it is modeled after, such as the Russell 2000 whose symbol is RUT.

Again we look to the **Research Wizard**. It directs you to the **Aim** or **Goal** of the fund. As you go through the **LINKS** you will see things like how many

Securities/stocks are in it by clicking on the **Top 25**. This is one of the short comings of owning just mutual funds. You money is spread thin. This makes growth slower and lower. If you owned 5 stocks with 1000 shares in each, you would earn $1000.00 each time that particular stock price goes up $1.00.

Mutual funds rarely grow more than a dollar a month. Occasionally one of special design like a tech fund will grow. But they never grow as fast as stocks themselves. My former financial advisor was the person who led me to invest in stocks. They pointed this out the short fall to me.

It is up to you to learn how to use the system. You may have noticed that you didn't receive a phone call telling you to switch your 401k fund around. The same thing applies to brokers. They will do what you ask them, but they will rarely suggest selling a stock unless you give them instructions to. But how can you give instructions, if you don't know what they are? Remember you are only one of a thousand clients. Unless you have a large account, don't expect special treatment. I'm assuming you will continue to look through the **Research Wizard**. It will help you tremendously. Click on some of the stocks and compare the growth of the stock to the fund itself.

Now click on **Returns.** As you can see 1999 was a banner year for this fund and most funds. Now you can see where following the Dow would have helped you preserve your gains. When it dropped in March 2000 you could have moved into another investment. In the charting section you will see it plain as day when this fund was decreasing in value.

Now click on **Top 25 Holdings.** These are the top 25 of the 145 stocks in this fund. To see the rest you would have to go to the website or read the dreaded Prospectus. Incidentally a mutual fund prospectus is a good place to shop for individual stocks.

To see what I mean about spread thin, click on a particular stock like **C** (Citigroup) which at this time is $38.54 a share(In 2002). Now the fund share price is at $ 33.91. Now say you bought 1 fund share today at $33.91. You would have to split up the $33.91 into 145 portions. This will give you approx..23 cents toward each share of the stocks in the fund. You are buying .23 cents worth of a $38.54 share of Citigroup which will take you 168 contributions @ .23 to own 1 share of Citigroup. So if you contribute bi-weekly it will take you about 6 years to buy 1 share, and that's provided the price doesn't go up, which Citigroup being a excellent company will certainly go up. Add to that five fees they charge you.

---

[4] Robbing you blind by Mark Dempsey

Bad as this sounds I am not knocking owning mutual funds. I once owned several (because I was forced to in my 401k), but they are not the best way to gain growth. Mutual funds are for people who want to pay minimum attention to what is going on in the market and haven't learned how to really take advantage of the system or you want to park a million dollars in a seemingly low risk investment. But if you owned one through 2000-2002 you saw that they aren't perfectly safe and that you do have to pay some attention. Because of the losses, some people started calling their 401k's a 201k. Again the purpose of this book is to help you gain control of your future and avoid loss. Click on the rest of the links on your own time.

Go to **WWW.NASDAQ.COM.** There are some basic things you need to know about this site. It will help you where other sites may not. This site has a glossary, insider trading list, a peek at the World Market, News and some free research. Also they offer research you have to pay for. I wouldn't start paying for anything until you have the basics understood and you plan to do some short term trading to make money. You have more than enough information to monitor long term investing for now.

Start with the **Quote** box on the left. You can look up 10 stocks at the same time. As a example[1] I'll use BVSN (Broadvision), HIV Calypte Biomedical, SGI (Silicon Graphics), and ELC (Electricity Corporation) in some of the 10 open boxes.

This is a cross breed of stocks from the NYSE (New York Stock Exchange), NASDAQ (National Association of Stock Dealers Automated Quotation) AMEX (American Stock Exchange and the OTCBB (Over the counter bulletin board). As a FYI, OTCBB stocks are never seen on the stock ticker. I have found profitable growing companies listed on the Bulletin board. One such company was

True religion (TRLG). Once they had become profitable the stock went from .79 to $15.00 in 9 months.

Start with Silicon Graphic (SGI) a NYSE stock. In the drop box click **Info Quotes.** Now click on **Holdings/ Insiders.** Click on the word **Total number of holders.** Note that there are 90 Institutional or brokerages that hold this particular stock. At the bottom of that section is a list of page numbers that allow you to see who these institutional holders are, how many shares they are handling and if they have sold them. (F.Y.I. Shares Outstanding are shares held by investors). Institutional holdings of a stock is a good sign.

Now let's do one of the more difficult stocks to research. HIV Calypte biomedical. This is commonly referred to as a penny stock. This is one of the few sites at present, that give you information on penny stocks.

Brokers call any stock under $5.00 a penny stock. But this is where you are most likely to gain the most growth. Microsoft used to be a penny stock selling at .15 cent a share. A $1500.00 investment in 1986 would have yielded $1,200,000.00 in January 2000 @ $120.00 a share. Did your mutual fund gain that much in the same period? I didn't think so. Your broker probably would have discouraged you from buying in at that price. Then they would call you when it hit $10.00 and recommend that you buy it. It was a good deal at $10.00 but it was better a .15 cents. If you're going to invest for the long term why not go for maximum growth?

Look at **Listed Companies** on the left lowewr portion of the screen**.** Now click on National Market list. You get a brief description of the company. If you click on the symbol you will get the price which in most cases, will be less than $5.00 a share.

Some other good sites to look at are **WWW.OTCBB.COM** and **WWW.OTCFN. COM**. Also you can look in the business section of **USA Today**. The have a list called **E-25**. There are some stocks priced under $5.00 a share. These are for long term investing. Something like 5 years or for your childrens college fund.

Back to Calypte. They have 5 institutions holding their stock at this time. This company has unique product. They can test for HIV by using urine. No blood test, nothing taken internally. China has recently began ordering this test (see news report MSN.COM 01-06- 03). All fifty American state insurance regulators have accepted them. This means that insurance companies may be using this service in the near future. No doubt this will protect them from long term medical bills.

They eventually will require companies that they insure, to test new employee applicants. They may even buy this company. Can you see the possibilities.

You will find that Over the Counter stocks receive little attention at the present. They are risky. In April of 2002 Calypte was threatening to close up shop. These stocks can get aborted at times so beware. Also, this company is a threat to companies that sell the blood test for HIV. Watch before you buy. Financial politics can get nasty. This company does fit 2 basic criteria **1. Large impact on a large segment of society. 2. Probability of a long period of sales**.

You can wait until companies like this graduate to another exchange like the AMEX or NASDAQ and stay above $1.00 a share. Above all make them a small portion of your portfolio until you get a handle on what's going on. If you click on **Help** at the bottom of the page, and then click on **Glossary** and go down to **Stock Symbols**. You will learn about the fifth letter on NASDAQ stocks and what it is telling you about the company. You can finish touring this site, I want to move on to where you can find out financial details on a penny stock.

Go to **WWW. SECINFO.COM.** Type in the company name. Calypte Biomedical and click **Search**. Sometimes when you are out riding and you see a truck with a sign on it, or you are going through a Mall and you see a potential store that may go national some day. You may be able to go here to find out info on them. If a friend invites you to a seminar and they are selling stock in a ground floor opportunity and you can't find them here it could be a scam. All public stock sold should be registered with the S.E.C. Security Exchange Commission. I know of people who were duped into buying stock in non-existent companies by **Family Members. This may not apply to privately held companies.**

Click on Calypte. Now before you get all frustrated, go back to **Fool.com.** In the search box type in Quarterly reports. Item no.4 should be **How to read a Balance sheet. (**If not then type in How to read a balance sheet.) You will find this easy to read. They also tell you what to look for so you don't have to read the entire report.

Now go back to the SEC site. Click on **Quarterly reports 10-Q.** Now click **10-Q** preferrably the latest report. Slide down the page and the numbers start showing up. I just wanted you to see where NASDAQ and other sites get their information.

The information on the SECINFO site comes from a database called **E.D.G.A.R.** (Eletronic Data Gathering, Analysis and Retrieval system). You can go to http://www.sec. gov/edgar. shtml for more information if you desire.

Now, let's look at one of the best ways to find a stock to invest in. Go to www.yahoo.com then click **Finance** on the top left. Now click on **screener** where it say's **Stock Research** on the left. You may have to download the java software.

First note the preset screens. It gives you a variety based on the type of investing you want to do. On this page click **more preset screens**. Now click on **Bargain growth.** One of the main reasons for choosing this particular screen is because *Institutional investors* is used as part of the search criteria. Because of the laws institutions have to abide by for investor protection. The amount of money they usually have invested makes it hard for them to just jump out of a stock with out being noticed. They avoid non-profitable companies. They generally stay with choices above $5.00 a share.

When the screen comes up, click on the next **Add criteria** button. When the box drops, click on **Share performance** then click **Current price.** Now add *Between* and then in the Value section put 5 and 50. This limits the price of our selection to those amounts. Now click **Run screens.** To make it easy look for the one that is positive across the board. You may want look up *Return on assets, Return on equity and Forward PE* at either Investopedia.com or Fool.com.

For this exercise I chose [5]Delta Petroleum symbol DPTR. Today's price is $10.89. I can see from the screen, which is positive across the board that this is a pretty good prospect. Let's look deeper. To set up a second page hit **ctrl** and the **n** button at the same time. Now go back to the MSN.COM /MONEY. (You can hit the F11 button on the top of your keyboard to get a full page. Hit again to return to the original size.) Starting in the top section the Revenue is $63 million.

The year over year Gross profit is steadily growing 15% a year, which is excellent. The Net profit is positive. Remember when you see parentheses that means negative. Now looks at the Ownership. This list the Major holders of the stock. This is also a good indicator of profitability. You want to see above 20% institutional ownership. (This stock went up $6.00 over the next 60 days). Follow through with charting.

Click on **more preset screens** for additional screens. It presents you with stocks screens based on the type of investing you want to do.

One of the things I like about this site is that it gives detailed explanation of things such as the search criteria the screen uses and the types of stocks such as big caps and small caps. Notice what it says about Bargain Growth stocks. "This screen searches for stocks with price earnings growth ratio (**PEG)** less than or equal to 0.5 and total debt to equity ratios of less than or equal to 0.5. It also looks for earnings growth estimates for the next five years of greater than or equal to 25%. Finally, it limits companies that have institutions holding greater than or equal to 20% of shares and sales for the past twelve months of greater than or equal to $100 million." In other words, companies with financial stability, and forward looking earnings prospects. Studying how the computer screens for stocks, will help you set up your own particular type of screen. You always want to pick companies that have the potential to make money in the future. Let's do a manual stock screen.

[5] This stock choice is only an example and is not to be assumed as a recommendation.

Click on **Yahoo finance screen** located on the first preset screen page. After a couple of pop-ups it should appear. You should see in green the words click to add criteria. Click on that and it should drop down. Click on **Income Statement.** Then on the flip-out and click **Net income.** Net income is the real money that's available. Over to the right you will see *Criteria Definitions.* Click on it if you want to read the actual definition of Net Income. Under **Conditions**, click **Between.** Under **Values** 2 boxes will appear. This is money amount. Click **10m** in the first one. In the second section click on the drop box and then click on 1b(billion).

Now click on click to add criteria at the next level. Click on **Valuation.** Then click on Forward P/E. Then click between and for values use 5 & 25. Now on the next level use **Share performance,** then **Moving average,** then **Last price up % 50 day moving average.** Then Condition(between), then for Values use .25 to 50.

Next use **Balance Sheet,** then **Cash per share**, Between, and for Values use 1 to 10. Next go back to Income statement, on the flip-out use EPS ( ttm = Twelve trailing months, or Earnings Per Share or how much money was left over for stock holders in the last 12 months.) Use Between and for Values use .10 as in ten cents to .25.

Next is **Cash flow**, use both Free cash flow and Operation cash flow. Condition>Between, 1m and 1b.

Now click **Run screen** over on the left near the middle of the page. You should have a pretty good potential list of candidates.

Now pick a price range. Go to[4] Bigcharts.com and check the 5 year/monthly chart to see how high your choice has been. Then compare it to it's present price. Run a 6 month/daily and study the price change pattern hi vs. low. At the least you will have a good swing trade candidate. If you see one that moves $1 to $5 every 1 to 3 months you might want to use it. Remember always buy at the 10 day/hourly low (below the support/resistance, lines crossing, pointing upward). If the stock has had 3 or 5 day run up, wait until it pull back in price. Later on I will show you how to trade these for a tenth of what they cost. So don't fret over the prices.

Go back to the main Finance page. On the right click on **Actives.** Then click on **Price % Gainers**. Here, no matter what the market is doing you can find stocks that are headed up on a down day. This is a good place to find short and long term candidates. Remember long term candidates require research.

Investor's Business Daily is a excellent time saving website. They are one of the best sites with some of best stock picks around. You might want to subscribe to their site. It is worth the money.

# Charting, the microscope and telescope of the Market

I can't emphasize enough that if you want to see when a stock reaches it's peak or bottom, if you want to know the perfect time to get into or out of a stock at the best price. **YOU MUST LEARN HOW TO READ CHARTS.**

I have excellent news for you this is the easiest part, and it is the most effective way to avoid loss and maximize gain. When you buy stock or invest in anything you should have an expectation of growth.

The purpose of investing is financial gain. You want to multiply what you have without losing it. All investments have risk. You can buy property, and a event not covered by insurance could happen. You could lose your entire investment. Property is one lawsuit a way from total loss. Near the end of this book I will be sharing on how to legally protect any investment from loss including I.R.S seizure and how to reduce your taxes. Remember **stocks never stay at their maximum price.** Be prepared to sell.

In the past charts were sent out in the mail, now you can see them on the Internet.

Go to **WWW.Bigcharts.com**. I want to start with long term investing. This is most likely the type of investing most people want to do. Charts draw pictures based on the actual buying and selling of a stock or mutual fund. This how you track or study the performance of a stock. You could read the numbers, but this is easier.

---

[6] Charting is covered in the next chapter

Type in **MSFT** in the search box, then click on **Interactive.** In the **Time** dropbox, click on **Custom**. The **Custom** box allows you to go back into a specific time frame to check a stock's movement on daily, weekly or monthly basis. For instance, if you want to see what happened on March 10, 2000 you can use this.

Set the **Year** 01/01/1986 to 02/01/1987. Set the **Frequency** at **Weekly**. Now click on **Indicators.** Set **Moving Averages** at **SMA 2 line with 50 (space) 200. (** Simple Moving Average**)**. Set the **Upper Indicator** on **Parabolic SAR** (Stop and Reversal). In the first **Lower Indicator** click **MACD** (Moving Average Convergence Divergence). In the second **Lower Indicator** click **Volume +.** In the third indicator, click **Slow Stochastics** (a momentum indicator)**.** Now click **Draw Chart.**

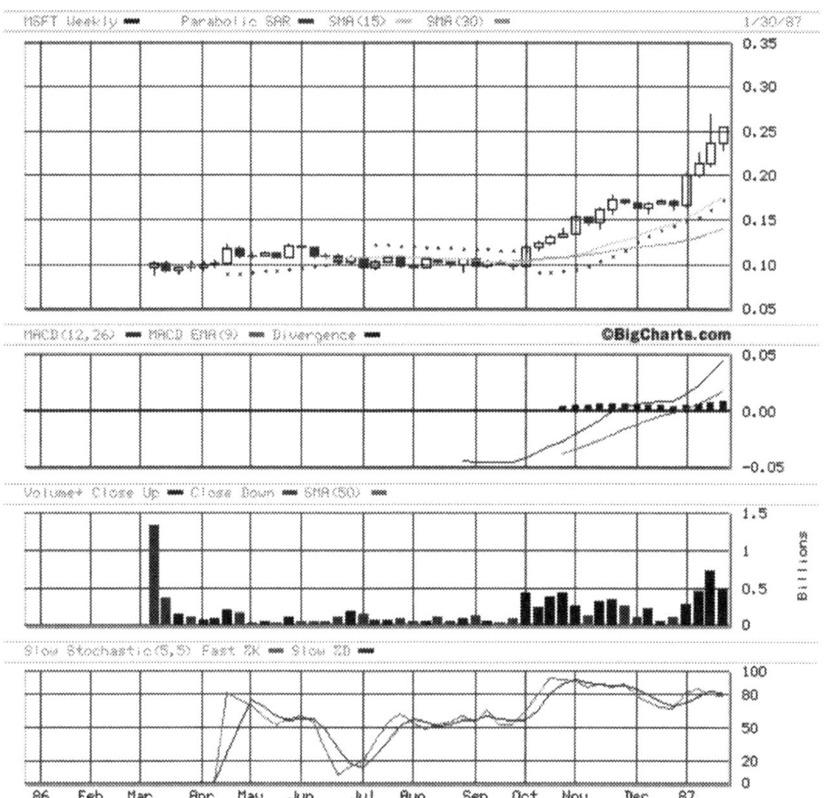


You can see where Microsoft began. This obviously would have been the best time to get the greatest gain. Computers were just beginning to become a household product. Now you see what I mean **Impact on society.** Again a $1500.00 investment back in 1986 would have netted $1,200,000.00 in December 1999. What if 10% of your 401k investment had of been Microsoft and you sold it December 1999? Now I will show you how you would have known to sell.

Change the **Time** to **1 Decade** and **Frequency** to **Monthly.** Now click **Draw charts.** In the Upper Indicator those **dots** change from being under the Candlesticks to being on top of the Candlesticks. The candlesticks represent what is called a

**Price line.** If you look to the right, you will see the price running along the edge of the chart. Draw a line from the top right of the candlestick to the price on the right. This is how you know the price for that period of time. If it is a daily price, that is the closing price for that day. If hourly, it' the price for that particular hour.

Whenever those dots change position, that's when the stock price is reversing ie. **Stop and Reversal**. When the dots are on the bottom the price is going up, and when they are on the top the price is going down. Note the lines where the arrow is pointing on the example. They cross in a coordinated move with the dots. When the lines cross each other the price is headed downward. In the Lower Indicator the same thing occurs when the **MACD** lines cross.

Notice the **black horizontal** line going horizontally across the **MACD** chart. That's called a **Support/ Resistance line**. Note the coordinated movement of the pegs on the line. The pegs are called a **Histogram**. The price goes up the pegs are on top and vice/versa. Generally you'd buy when the stock or mutual fund it is below the support/resistance line using a 10 day/hourly chart, and sell when the lines go upward to what would appear to be its peak and cross.

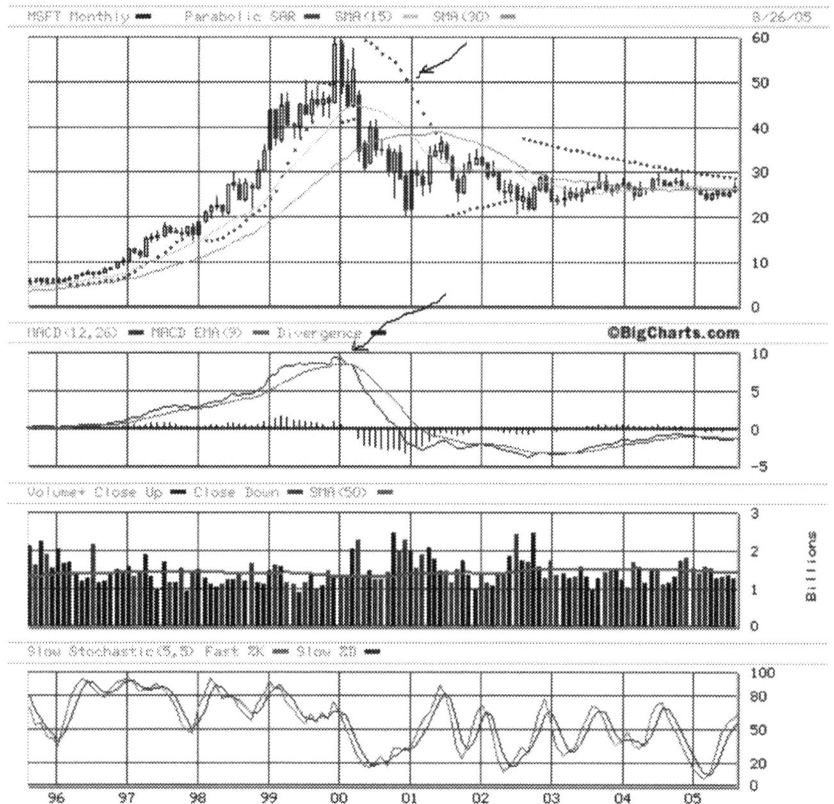


Use a (**Time**)3-5 year (**Frequency)** monthly time frame for long term. The **MACD** is the easiest to follow especially for long term.

You do want make sure that the 50 and 200 day moving average lines are below the price indicators on that top chart. When the price drops below 50 and 200 day average and the MACD lines are pointing downward, you may want to pull out. The market may be going through a minor correction (decrease in average). Pay attention to the NASDAQ chart. Watch the 6 month/daily. Watch the lines go down cross, turn up and separate. Then you can get back in.

I do what is called swing trading I may trade once over a 1 to 60 day period to reach my objective. When those lines go up past the support/resistance line and look like they are going to cross and head down, I'm out. I may either wait until it drops below the support /resistance and cross and head up or move on to another stock that is breaking out in a similar fashion. I use a 10 day/hourly and 6 month daily for this.

In a break out (the price is about to shoot up) the Moving Average lines turn upward and separate and head past the **Support/ Resistance line.** This effect is seen during any time frame you choose to trade, short or long term. For long term trading use **1-2 year/weekly** time frame. For medium I use **6 Month/daily.** I use the 50 and 200 SMA. For short term trading look at and **10 day/hourly.** Change the **SMA** to **15 50.** Just before buying look at the **1 Day/ 5 minute and then 1 minute** to get the best price you can. Always buy after a price pull-back (slight recline) on the 10 day/hourly. Stocks usually pull back after a 3 to 5 day run-up.

You should make a list of about 40 stocks to follow on a regular basis. You can make a list at the MSN.COM, Yahoo/finance or AOL/quote site. You must register at MSN and then you can click on **Portfolio.** This will allow you to add the stocks you are following. It is free to register at all the sites. If you watch Mad Money you will have 40 excellent stocks.

The other 2 indicators help gage the strength level or activity level that is going on, such as strong selling or buying. In the **Volume+** the Red is Bearish/ Selling and Black is Bullish/ Buying. The **Slow stochastic** measures overbought and oversold conditions. When a stock is over-bought it is likely to go down in price. Oversold does the opposite.

Overbought and oversold conditions should be viewed on the **6 month/daily.** Note the position of the price line in relation to the 50 and 200 day MA lines on the Parabolic SAR chart. They should be heading upward. It is ideal if the price line is above them. That indicates continual buying. This is significant when a stock approaches or pass it's 52 week high. If the forward earnings are good, this could indicate a higher high.

Above each **Indicator** section is a hyper-link . If you click on it, it will give you more information about a particular chart.

If you go to **Stockcharts.com** and click on **Chart School** you will get more information. At the Stockcharts.com site over on the top-right is quote box and a drop-box. Use **Gallery view**. Note the 50 and 200 day moving average lines. They are usually red and blue. This will help you in determining which way the stock is headed in near term. If the 200 day is moving down you can pretty much count that the stock price is going down also. That might make a good candidate for a long [7]Put option.

Over on the left is a list of hyper-links. Click on **Stockscans.** A list of potential trades will come up. One of my favorites is **Oversold with improving RSI (relative strength indicator).** Oversold stocks with good fundamentals, tend to go back up. Now click the number listed under NASDAQ. You see the small pictures, click on the third one going from left to the right.

On the top is a MACD chart. Below is Candlestick chart. This is a 6 month/daily view. Most charts show the beginning of a upward breakout (lines crossing heading upward.) Again use a 10 day/hourly etc. before buying a stock. This site won't let you create a 10 day chart unless you subscribe for full service, which is worth it, if you want my opinion.

---

[7] Put options are discussed later.

If you click on **Chart School** and then click on **Chart analysis** you can learn about Candlesticks and what their pattern mean.

This is where the money is. You can find stocks, but getting the most gain out of them is right here. Most traders works with charts. Everyone that I know that has lost money in the Stock market, not one of them told me they used charts. Most didn't know they existed. They were gambling. Trying to guess in the dark or relying on their broker. **Charts take the blinders off**.

You can chart the NASDAQ (**IXIC**) the Dow (**INDU**) or any market indicator. As a matter of fact if you chart the NASDAQ back to 1999 from the present, you will notice all the selling (red) on the **Volume+** section in 2000 and in 2003 you will see the buying (black).

Knowing the general direction of the market is essential, in making buying and selling decisions. Also Bigcharts.com will allow you to e-mail charts to yourself as a reminder. Just look at the bottom of the page.

This is the Computer age. Computers provide a great advantage to investors. Charts get their information from the actual buying and selling of stocks. The computer Chart program does the calculations for you. For instance in the **Upper indicator (Bigcharts.com)** drop box click on **Earnings.** Now you're looking Microsoft's quarterly earnings for the last 10 years in a picture. This saves you hours of reading time and using calculators. Is this making any sense? Are you beginning to see that it is easier to invest online than you thought? Does it deserve a little of your time?

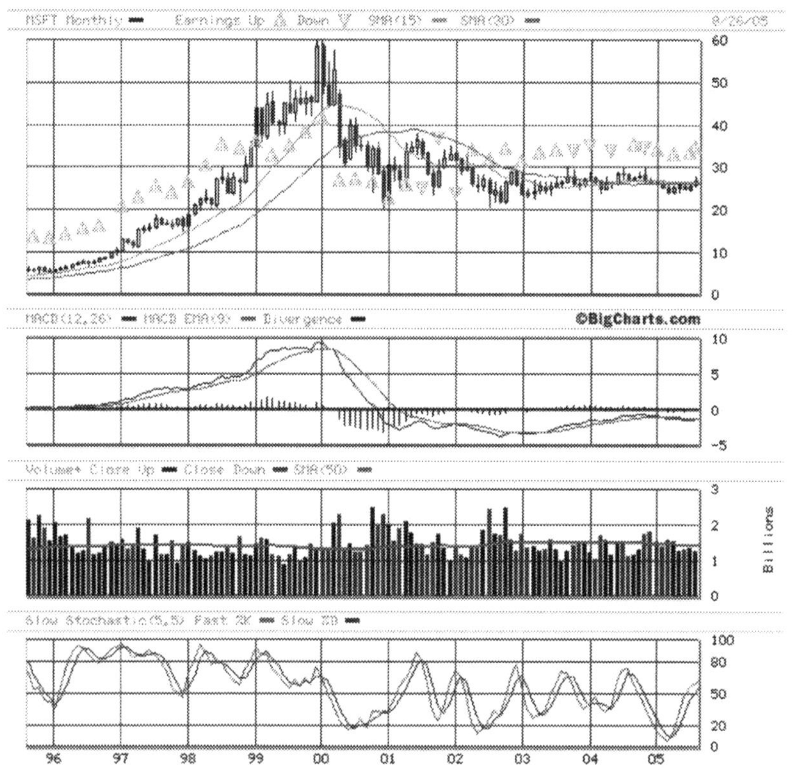


This same chart system can be used for a mutual funds. Put **JAWWX** (Janus Worldwide) in the box. Use a **Decade/ monthly** time frame**.** Notice the same effect occurs. The lines cross, the price drop. At that time you would move into a Bond fund or any **Guaranteed** portion of your mutual fund group. You can stay there Collcct 3 6% on your gains until the Market turns, rather than loose what you gained. Your broker or financial advisor probably never called you, while your money was depreciating. They probably watched these charts, as it was going down. But again, it isn't totally their responsibility. Ask them.

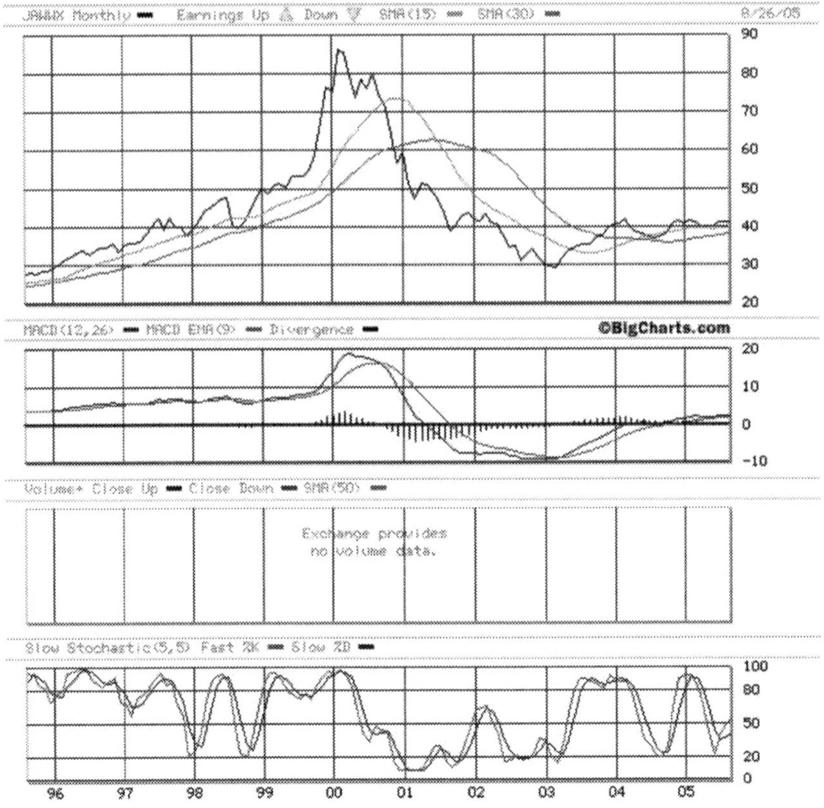
JAWWX Monthly Earnings Up Down SMA(15) SMA(30)
8/26/05
90
80
70
60
50
40
30
20
MACD(12,26) MACD EMA(9) Divergence
©BigCharts.com
20
10
0
-10
Volume+ Close Up Close Down SMA(50)
Exchange provides
no volume data.
Slow Stochastic(5,5) Fast %K Slow %D
100
80
50
20
0
96
97
98
99
00
01
02
03
04
05

**IXIC** Nasdaq Composite Index 8/26/2005

| NAV: | Change: | Offer: | Yield: |
|---|---|---|---|
| **2,120.77** | **-13.60** | **2,133.17** | **n/a** |
| | Percent Change: | | 52 Week Range: |
| | **-0.64%** | | **1,819.62 to 2,219.91** |

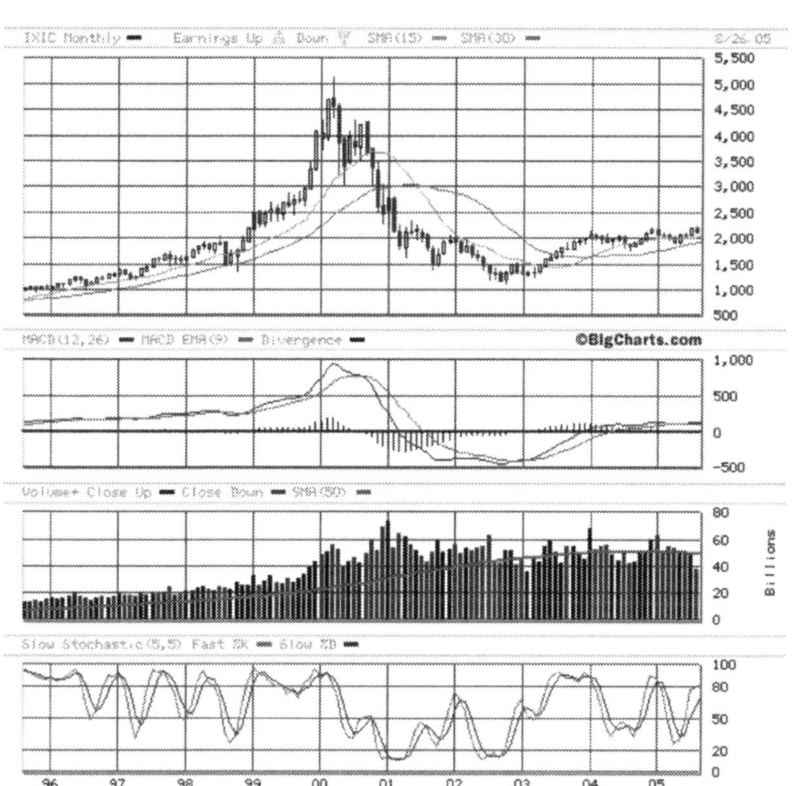

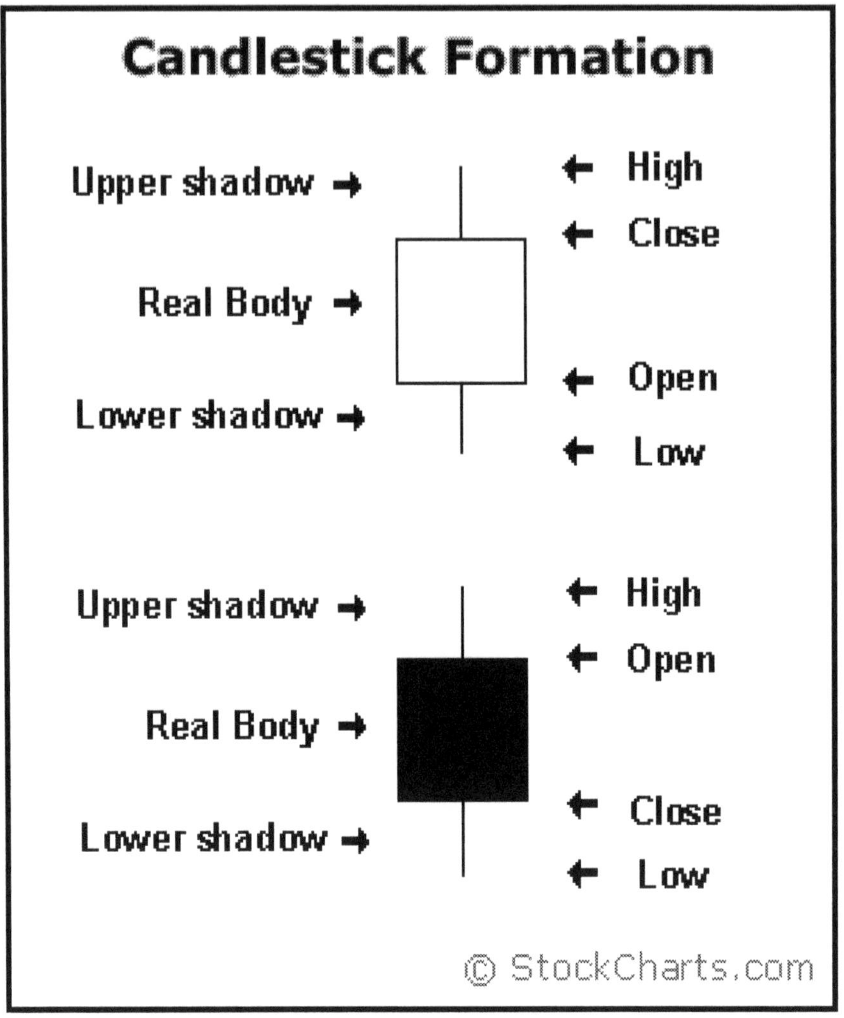
Candlestick Formation
Upper shadow
High
Close
Real Body
Open
Lower shadow
Low
Upper shadow
High
Open
Real Body
Close
Lower shadow
Low
© StockCharts.com

## Simple Investment Strategies

You can count on this being simple. These methods have helped me grow 70% in 2003 without adding money. I'm assuming that if you bought this book you are not trying to be a daytrader. However, you are interested in improving your investments using the internet. So I will begin with long term strategies.

To me it is not to my best interest to tie up money for several years, only to see a 10% gain, especially when I can get 10,000 %. How much you will get is dependent on your risk level and willingness to do a little research. If you pay attention to the investment tools I have already shown you, you will reduce your risk level and research time. Also you will no longer be buying blind.

The first method is the **buy and hold**. That's how Warren Buffet made his billions. The key is to pick the right product. Remember that statement **Impact on society?** Along with that add **how much of society will be affected? for what period of time,** and **strong balance sheet**. Never invest long term in companies that aren't generating positive income.

Microsoft is a good example. They along with IBM and Intel made computers available for the average home. I remember seeing another computer company long before I even heard of Microsoft but they were unable to get to the general public with the ease that Microsoft did. The need for the product in the future, and the company's willingness to meet the need of the public will determine their long term profitability. But even with that knowledge the situation is subject to change. So keep your eye on the charts.

Let's say for example you looked at a company like Cyberads (CYAD). What draws your attention to this company? They have primary North American marketing rights over the new X-Board. This is a surfboard with a 40 h.p. rotary engine. Because it is an OTCBB (Bulletin Board) stock you would run the company through the **SECINFO.COM** and **NASDAQ.COM** site.

This is also a company that is changing it's business model. They are focusing on xtreme sports equipment. That is crucial because they are entering in to uncharted waters. How you conduct business for one type of product or service is different than that of another. In other word's, how you sell shoes is different from how you sell furniture. On the plus side adding new income streams will help raise the stock price. That way the company isn't dependent on 1 product for income.

In Dec 2002 CYAD is at .03 cents a share. Holding it will be determined by observing the financial reports and what is going on with the market and the world at the time. The goal for growth is to $10.00 a share. This could take 5 to 10 years. This could be less, could be longer. The key is that I am only tying up $300.00 for 10,000 shares which will net me $100,000.00 @ $10.00 a share.

This is one caution note I must make. Sometime company's seek to trade on the NASDAQ ticker. In order to do so, they must improve their financial status and get the stock up above $1.00 a share and remain there. The company may do a reverse split of the stock. That means a 1 to 10 reverse split will reduce 10,000 share to 1000. If I have confidence in this company going forward because of good financial reports, I would continue buying this one stock until I have at least 10,000 to compensate for splits. The best opportunity is when the company buys back the stock.

The reduction in shares available is supposed to increase the stock price. The less available, the more traders have to pay to own it.

Don't buy it all at once. You should observe their development. **Read** news reports in the **Quote** section online and watch the charts. Visit **secinfo.com** once every 90 days. Watch the company news as well as the price of the stock. If the price jumps and there is no major news announcement, the jump was probably caused by stock speculators (people who bid the price up and sell for a quick profit). You could sell some and buy more when the price comes back down, but don't really focus on that. But if it has crossed it's 52 week high it could be making a move upward. The rule is, when a stock crosses it's 52 week high there are more buyers than sellers. Most companies don't go months without reporting news. They are in business to make money. They know investors want to know what is going on.

Next strategy is **Swing Trading or Core trading**. It is similar but the time period for holding is shorter. There is no intention to hold for a long period of years. These stocks are usually NASDAQ or NYSE stocks. This when you can use the CNBC ticker, stockscan or screener.

When the Tech bubble burst a lot of good companies got caught in the vacuum. Companies like Broadvision (BVSN), Webmethod (WEBM), Ariba (ARBA), Akamai (AKAM), Compuware (CPWR), Human Genome Sciences (HGSI) Ford Motor co. (F), and Oracle (ORCL) came down from prices as high as $345.00 a share. If you watch these companies they tend to go up and down about a $1.50. The goal in Swing trading is to make money for other long term investments or just becoming wealthy.

The holding period is 10 to 60 days. If you begin with $100.00, look for a stock that trades from $5.00 to $15.00. Stocks have a **15 day, 50 day and 200 day averages**. Averages reveal how the price changes during those periods. In those time periods they may only move up $1.00 a share. That's all you want. The goal is simply to make the $100.00 into $200.00. Once you have accomplished this repeat the process. Then make the $200.00 become $400.00. You may even trade the same stock more than once, especially if it's moving up and down in a pattern. Following is a chart to show you the benefits of putting effort into learning this method. (> = becomes)

1. 100>200
2. 200>400
3. 400>800
4. 800>1600
5. 1600>3200
6. 3200>6400
7. 6400>12800
8. 12800> 25,600
9. 25,600> 51,200
10. 51,200> 102,400
11. 102,400> 204, 800
13. 204,800> 409,600
14. 409,600> 819,200
15. $1,638,400

In 15 100% trades (Each trades makes 100% of the amount traded) you might be debt free, depending on how much debt you have. During a fluid Bull market (lot of active trading) it is highly possible.

As your skill level increase you will be able to make money in a Bear Market (down) by trading options or shorting a stock. An excellent book on option trading is **Trade Options online by George Fontanills ISBN 0-471-35938-6**. Option trading allow you to make the same amount of money even when the price is going down by buying what are called **PUT options**.

## Option trading basics 101

This is a little about Option trading. First let me say, to go further than what I am going to tell you, you must get training. You might want to contact Startrader.com. and find out when they will be near your area. If they aren't coming in your area, just look up **Option trading seminars** on Yahoo.com.

Okay, let's go back to Bigcharts.com. You should know how to put in a stock symbol by now.

To get an idea of the advantage of option trading let's use a frequently moving high priced stock. Now remember trading is for short term ownership, not long. The longest a option can held is a year.

Now type in the symbol for ebay, which is you guessed it EBAY. As you can see it is [8]$34.00 a share. Now just above the stock price info is 6 hyper-links. Click on **Option Chain.**

What you are looking at is, is the **premium** or **the price you pay** times 100 to control 100 shares of eBAY. Notice how significantly lower the premium price is. Instead of paying $34.00 plus dollars a share, you can **control** 100 shares for $340.00. In other words, instead of paying or putting at risk $3400.00

[8] This price is in July 2005

for 100 shares, you pay $340.00 to control 100 shares. If your premium increases a dollar you make $100.00 profit because you control 100 shares (minus trading fees.). You risk less for the same gain.

On the left side are **Call option** prices. These are for **buyers who believe the price of the stock is going up**. On the right is **Put options**, theses are **for buyers who believe that the stock price is going down**. You actually get paid a profit for a stock going down. You will also notice the bid (price you sell for) and the ask price (price you pay). **There** is also **Open int**, which is Open Interest. This is the number of options open. The higher the better. A lot of open interest could show the direction the stock is most likely to go.

I have to say that some stocks can increase under low volume. So volume doesn't always show growth. As a matter of fact, I have seen stocks grow $3 or $4 dollars in one day on low volume many times.

Going down the center is the **Strike Price**. This is the price you pick to begin profitability. Notice that it only has certain amounts and not every dollar amount. Usually 2.50 difference to 5.00.

To begin, **you must understand trading basics**. You must know charting. Choose only companies with good fundamentals.

You must learn the option language, such as **Buy to open** and **Sell to close**. This is the most basic trade.

Investopedia.com can help you here. Let's examine the roll of the **Strike Price**. Basically, the strike price(plus the premium price) is where your option becomes profitable. The actual point that a option becomes profitable is when the underlying stock price, plus the premium price added together is reached.

I must also add that you must deduct the trade fee for the option, which is the regular trade fee plus .75 per contract( at Ameritrade). So a trade fee for 10 contracts is $7.50+10.99= 18.49. They take the trade fee as soon as the trade is completed.

For instance, if the strike price is $33.00 and the premium price is $3.30 the actual price that the option becomes profitable is $36.30.

Once the stock price increases past the strike+premium price, you start making money. So, you want make sure that the 52 week high is past that amount. Because if it isn't you aren't likely to reach profit- ability with the Call option at that price, but you may profit from the Put option if the stock price starts heading downward.

Wait until the stock price comes down if it has been on a run up. You always want to buy on the pull back in price. The good part is that the premium price comes down.

One trade scenario is to use a lower strike price. This will have a higher premium. What you would do is, calculate which strike price +premium will put you closer to profitability.

For example if the stock price is $33.00 you would look at strike price such as $27.50, which has a premium of $7.80. This option would be profitable at $34.20 vs. $36.30. ($27.50+ $7.80 vs. $33.00+$3.30) At 33.00 you can see easily that I will reach profit- ability sooner at $34.20, rather than wait until it reaches $36.30. Buying in this manner is called buying "**In the money**." Other terms are **Out of the money** and **At the money .**

## In the money[9]

1. For a Call option, the option's strike price is below the market price of the underlying asset. In the money options will appear in the shaded area.
2. For a Put option, when the strike price is above the market price of the underlying asset.

Again, I want to stress that Options are for **Short Term trading.** These are not stocks you can hold for your grandchildren. The maximum time you can hold one is 1 year. You must make yourself aware of trading patterns or ups and downs of a particular stock. This is where charting comes in. It's the easiest way to see the pattern.

Start trading **on paper**. Write down the date, stock price, strike price and the premium price that is listed 90 days from today. You always want to give yourself 60 to 90 days to reach profitability. Do a daily price check to see what your gains or losses are. This will help you see where you will gain without risking any money.

If you happen to pick a stock that is steadily gaining and you want to stay with it, roll or sell (sell to close) the option you are in. Pick the same strike price of a option that is 60-90 days away. That way you can continue to make money. So if you have a September 17.50 and you are approaching the end of August, purchase the December or January 17.50. Remember buy on the pull back. There may be a difference in the price, but if you think it's worth it staying with buy it. You'll make up the difference. Set your stop loss/market at about 10% if it's short term and 30% if it's long.

---

[9] At Investopedia.com, type in, In the money.

Do both Calls and Puts. You can use Puts when the market enters a down cycle. You can use a Put for insurance case you aren't sure which direction the stock is going to go. A Put works the opposite of a Call. This gains value if a stock price goes down. This also what a Short does. Yeah I know your financial advisor or broker never even hinted that it is possible.

To set it up is the same. Look at the strike price and the premium price for the Put. Same rule applies. When it hit's the strike price+ the premium is when it becomes profitable. You really should want to learn this, but don't guess at it, get a good under standing.

George Fontanills book Trading Options Online, Investopedia.com and a good seminar will get you started. I am not going to re-invent the wheel here, there is a lot of books on the subject and there are more and more seminars being taught such as Star Trader.com ( It's the cheapest beginners course). With Options a little money can make some serious gain. **You must master charts and research**.

Buying and selling is basically the same, the language is somewhat different. Again **GET TRAINING.** It will be money well spent.

Okay let's do a run through this to help you understand.

**Step 1. Find a stock**. Use the Yahoo stock screener, or most active list, IBD 100, or go to Stockcharts.com and use the stock scan etc.

**Step 2. Review the financial history of the stock using Yahoo and MSN.com.** Read news reports, look at earnings reports. If you plan to hold it for more than 10 days you want to look at debt ratio, EPS, and cash availability more closely. This will get easier with practice.

**Step 3. Set your choice up on Bigcharts.com.** The longer the time you want to hold it, the further back you want to look. Note, sometimes you may want you want to look back a decade (decade /monthly) to see if the stock has a potential to go higher than the 52 week high. In a possible retracement (going back to it's highest price) it may go back to within 20 to 50% of it's highest high. It's possible, but not law, like Kmart. The company would have to grow its finances. Check the 6 month/daily, with 50 200 in the moving average box. Check the direction of both MA lines. They should be swinging up and separating. The MACD lines should be pointing up and away from each other. Check the 10 day/hourly chart with 15 50 MA. Remember you want the 10 day/hourly to have gone **down past the support/ resistance line , cross and point upward away from each other before you buy.** This effect is usually seen after a small pull back. Remember to look always to 1 hour/min. on Ameritrade to get the best price (for you penny pinchers ☺ ) Always make Limit orders.

**Step 4. Click on the option chain above.** Look at the strike price in relation to the Stock price. Remember the closer the strike price is to the stock price the sooner you reach profitability. For example if the Stock price is $32.00. The price movement history show a travel pattern of $32.00 to $40.00 in 30-60 days. You consider the lower strike price $30.00 option with a premium of $2.20. This will give you profitability at $32.20. Or you can buy the higher $32.50 option with a premium of $1.25 (32.50+1.25 Profitability@ $33.75). Remember to pick a option at least 60-90 days from the present date. If it is June, pick October options, not August. You want time to be your friend. Remember options expire every 3rd Friday. So this will give you until the 3rd Friday in October. You can choose January and maybe even a January LEAPS (**Long term Equity Anticipation Securities**) which is a year.

**Step 5. Make the trade.** For this example I am going to use Ameritrade. (This where my account is.) Click the **Trade** Button on the top dark blue line and then click on Options. Now check Buy to open. Now enter 1 in the contract # box. 1 contract controls 100 shares. Enter the option symbol, limit order, [10]price( I generally use the present Ask price ). So if your option increases from $2.20 to $4.20 in the time period you will have made $200.00 profit off a $220.00 investment. Roughly a 90% return.

Now remember when it comes time to sell you enter **Sell to close**. Also remember if you do this on paper, you can fearlessly trade as much as you want. I would suggest some 10 contract **paper trades** to see how fast money can grow. Plus you can set up a IRA account to do this in and never pay capital gains taxes. If you withdraw before age 59 ½ you will have to pay State and Federal taxes.

[10] Premium price is always multiplied by 100

OPTION CHAIN FOR EBAY INC

| CALLS | | | | | | | | PUTS | | | | | | |
|---|---|---|---|---|---|---|---|---|---|---|---|---|---|---|
| Hide September, 2005 Options | | | | | | | | | | | | | | |
| Symbol | Last | Change | Vol | Bid | Ask | Open Int. | StrikePrice | Symbol | Last | Change | Vol | Bid | Ask | Open Int. |
| QXBIB | 16.50 | | 10.00 | 16.40 | 16.70 | 11.00 | **22.50** | QXBUB | | | | | 0.05 | |
| QXBIE | 14.00 | | 10.00 | 13.90 | 14.10 | 10.00 | **25.00** | QXBUE | 0.10 | | 13.00 | 0.05 | 0.05 | 13.00 |
| QXBIC | 14.10 | | 10.00 | 11.40 | 11.60 | 16.00 | **27.50** | QXBUC | 0.05 | | 1.00 | 0.10 | 0.05 | 255.00 |
| XBAIF | 9.30 | | 1.00 | 9.00 | 9.10 | 199.00 | **30.00** | XBAUF | 0.05 | | 2.00 | 0.30 | 0.05 | 1,061.00 |
| XBAIZ | 6.40 | -0.10 | 1.00 | 6.50 | 6.70 | 136.00 | **32.50** | XBAUZ | 0.05 | -0.05 | 40.00 | 0.05 | 0.05 | 1,908.00 |
| XBAIG | 4.20 | +0.10 | 183.00 | 4.10 | 4.30 | 2,576.00 | **35.00** | XBAUG | 0.10 | -0.05 | 26.00 | 0.05 | 0.10 | 5,454.00 |
| XBAIU | 2.00 | -0.05 | 701.00 | 1.95 | 2.05 | 3,826.00 | **37.50** | XBAUU | 0.40 | -0.15 | 622.00 | 0.40 | 0.45 | 6,427.00 |
| | | | | | | Stock Price ▸ | 38.97 | Last as of 8/26/2005 4:00:00 PM | | | | | | |
| XBAIH | 0.70 | | 4,096.00 | 0.65 | 0.70 | 19,444.00 | **40.00** | XBAUH | 1.55 | -0.22 | 595.00 | 1.55 | 1.60 | 12,590.00 |
| XBAIV | 0.15 | -0.10 | 298.00 | 0.15 | 0.20 | 24,883.00 | **42.50** | XBAUV | 3.60 | -0.20 | 81.00 | 3.50 | 3.70 | 4,775.00 |
| XBAII | 0.10 | -0.05 | 64.00 | 0.05 | 0.10 | 15,383.00 | **45.00** | XBAUI | 5.90 | -0.30 | 40.00 | 5.90 | 6.10 | 985.00 |
| XBAIW | 0.05 | | 100.00 | 0.05 | 0.05 | 7,007.00 | **47.50** | XBAUW | 8.00 | | 6.00 | 8.40 | 8.60 | 70.00 |

Show October, 2005 Options
Show January, 2006 Options
Show April, 2006 Options
Show January, 2007 Options
Show January, 2008 Options

You can track options on Yahoo/finance.com. On the left of the quote page you will see a option hyper-link.

Stocks $30.00 and up tend to trade more frequently up and down. Many times they move $3.00 to $5.00 a share over a 20 to 60 day period. Trading options will make this more affordable.

To accomplish this you have to know the trading range of a stock. If you note the example of United Healthcare (UNH) and True Religion (TRLG) you can see the range of movement is about $1.00 every 30 days.

The website **Channelingstocks.com** focuses on looking for stocks that move in this manner. If you decide to go this way **Please get training or be extremely observant.** It will be well worth it. Look up Startrader.com or Teach me to trade.com. Findout when they will be in your area.

You will have to learn how to use **Limit, Stop market limit or loss and Trailing limits**. Once you've signed up with a broker such as Ameritrade, E-trade, T.D. Waterhouse or Scottrade there will be a page where all the transactions take place. The purpose of the **Limit** is to allow you the ability to program the computer to buy and sell stock or option at a set price. If you don't set a price, depending which online broker you choose you may not get the very best price.Sometimes a few pennies can make a difference. When there is no set price you wind up paying **Market** price. If you've observed the Stock market, you will notice that stocks will go up in the first few minutes of trading and come back down, go back up around noon and come back down and some times go back up or down towards the end of the day. Watching charts will clearly point this out. Avoid chasing a stock price and wait for it to execute.

**Stop market limits/loss** and **Trailing limits/stops** help prevent you from losing all your investment when you aren't paying attention. A **Stop market limit/loss** is a set price that you want the stock sold at if it began to decline in price. For instance let's say you bought VALinux (LNUX) at $2.00 and in one year climbed to $8.00. You would set a **Stop market limit** at $7.00.If the stock drops to $7.00 the computer would sell the stock. This leaves you with a 200+ % gain. Yes it could turn right around and go back up but odds are it will come back down.

As time goes on you will become a good judge on what to do. I would suggest setting a **Stop market limit at 20%**. Now suppose the stock goes up to $12.00 but comes back down to $8.00. You haven't loss anything but you missed an opportunity to make more.

That's where **Trailing limits/stop** comes in. You can set a **Trailing limit/stop** by cash amount or percentage. The difference is when you set the **Trailing limit/stop** it follows the stock price up. In the same scenario as above you get a better selling opportunity when it goes to $12.00. A 10 % **Trailing limit/stop** would sell the stock at $10.80. I only set trailing limits when I expect a surge in the market and the charts show that the stock may go back down in price and I may not be able to keep an eye on it. This allows me to take advantage of 25% gains that often. You can use trailing limits with options at this time.

Another method is to buy 2000 shares @ $2.00 a share. You hold it to $12.00 a share. The 10 point/dollar increase made you $10,000.00. Now repeat this process with the $10,000.00. You have $50,000.00. Guess how much you net with next trade? Look at the average 401k after 10 years. You can beat it in the same time span using this method. You have plenty of time to find the next stock to move to.

One other method is called using a **buying range**. The goal is to buy a large number of shares, say 25000. A stock that is presently $1.00 a share, set a buy range or continue to purchase the same stock until it reaches the price of $5.00. This allows me time to accumulate shares. This would be a stock that is expected to grow over a 5 to 10 year period at least $50.00 a share like Taser did. I may even go beyond the $5.00 buy limit to $10.00 primarily because of my expectation. Which of course is based on good company performance. Now, let's say at $5.00 I have accomplished my goal of 25000 shares. From this point on every time the stock goes up a dollar I receive $25000.00. This means at $15.00 my investment has grown $250,000.00, with out adding additional money.

For example a company like XM, Sirius satellite radio. Do you think it is fad or that it is the radio of the future? What do you think will happen with the stock price as market exposure increases and sale increase? If every car in the world eventually has satellite radio, do you think the value of their stock will go up. The American auto companies and some rental car companies are already offering it in their cars. Will this increase market exposure?

Companies like these are ones I would use this method for. **A large impact on, a large segment of society, for a long period.** Their balance sheet is a little shakey right now, but that added income from the auto companies will help that.

Note, there have been some changes in the tax law. If you trade stocks held less than a year, the gains are treated as income from a second job or business. You are taxed at your regular tax rate. If you hold stock for more than a year you pay the higher capital gains rate. The capital gains rate however lowers each year the stock is owned. It hits its minimum if held 5 years. It can go as low as 8%. You can talk with tax professional.

## Paper trading exercise 10-3-2005

This is a **PAPER** trading exercise, which means you do it on paper and not with real money. This allows you to mess up for free.

This exercise covers a 4 month period. This will be a **OPTIONS TRADING.** I will using both **In the money and Out of the money** options so that you can see the difference.

Any term that you don't understand, go to www.investopedia.com or www.fool.com . Type in the term and receive you answer. If that fail send me a email @ Investorhelp@comcast.net. I will explain what it is you don't understand.

Alright, let's get down to business. You should have some type of a note book that you can keep a record. Either a book form or use the excel portion of your Microsoft word or Linux.

You want to put the basics like date , stock symbol, stock price, Option expiration month, strike price, premium price, and number of contracts across the top of the page.

Remember that options **ALWAYS** come in 100 shares per contract. So 10 contracts, equal 1000 shares. 100 contracts is 10000 (ten thousand for those of you who have been out school for a while ☺.)

Math is real important, so keep your calculator handy. While I'm, here I want you note that when you have 10000 shares, if the premium moves up .10/cents you gain $1000.00 .

Ok now that you've set up your note book go to www. Bigcharts.com or yahoo/finance.com. These are the symbols we will be using. (Use any regular traded stock at the time.)

DELL- Dell computer 9-23-05 Stock price 34.09

Option- Jan 06 Call # 1 DLQAF Strike- $30.00. Premium $5.00 ( **ITM** In the money) 2 contracts. Invested $1000.00 Actual price $6818.00@ 34.09 for 200 shares.

Sell Strike price pass $39.00. Place Stop loss at 20% below the premium, which is $4.00

# 2 Call-DLQAT Strike- 37.50 Prem. .75 ( **OTM** Out of the money) 3 contracts. Invested .$225.00 Actual price 300 shares @ 34.09 $10227.00

Sell when strike price hits $39.00, Stop loss at .65

Nov. Put #3 contracts -DLQWG Strike- 35.00Prem. 1.75 **ITM** . 5 contracts. Invested $875.00 vs $17045.00

Stop loss @ 1.50

SIRI- Sirius satellite radio. Stock Price $6.70

Jan 06 Call QXOIA Strike 6.00. Premium 1.25 **ITM** 10 contracts

Invested $1250.00 vs. $6700.00 Stop loss @1.15

Jan 06 Call QXOAU Strike 7.50Premium .60 **OTM** 10 contracts

Invested. $600.00 vs. $6700.00 Stop loss @ .50

Dec 05 PUT QXOXI Strike 6.00 Premium.35 **OTM** 10 contracts

Invested $350.00 vs $6700.00

Sell or place stop loss after $.30

If you were actually setting this up, depending on which way you most expect the stock price to go, you would use a 20% stop loss to minimize loss on either the Call or the Put.

Remember, the Call pays when the Stock price goes up and the Put pays when the price goes down.

Set up a 1 year/weekly chart for DELL. You will notice it has a $33.00 low and a $40.00 high. It is at it's low area, However Rita and her evil sister Katrina has effected it's return or retrace. The is the purpose of the Put. If for a unexpected reason the stock suddenly drops in price it will grow $500.00 for every $1.00 drop in stock price.

(It actually did drop to 31.50 after a Greenspan statement)

Plus if you put in the 20% Stop market/loss on the Call, it will sell at the set price of $4.00. This will save your investment and make you money at the same time.

This why I recommend, that you get training. Options have a lot of benefits, but require experience. The big plus is even when the Market is headed down you can make money. This is why I want you learn on paper first. So you can see how the premium prices change in relation to the Stock Price.

I chose DELL because it is financially sound and is presently the leader in computer sales. As you can see by the chart I expect it to return to its 52 week high.

I chose Sirius because of Howard Stern, Mel Karmizin and the development of Satellite TV specifically XM and Sirius. Howard Sterns debut should cause a $2.00 dollar increase in the next couple of months as 2006 approach.

You can also check option prices at the Yahoo finance page. It's located right under Quotes. Just click on the word Option.

## Some helpful retirement information.

There are different types of retirement investment systems today. One of the most common is the **401k and Individual Retirement Account (IRA).** In January 2006 there will be a 401k Roth.

Presently there are two types of IRA'S, the **Traditional** and the **Roth**. You can use these for your children also. Depending on where you get your IRA will determine what types of investing you can do. **You want to be sure that they allow you to buy your own selection of stocks or mutual funds.**

**The 401k** allows you to save $13,500 a year. The Traditional IRA allows you (if you qualify) a tax write-off up to $3000.00 for a single person and $6000.00 for married people a year. Because it is a tax deferred (meaning you pay taxes when you spend it later) investment vehicle, you have to pay State and Federal taxes when you withdraw from it before the age of 59 1/2. You don't pay capital gains tax after retirement. There is a penalty of 10% for early withdrawals of principal if the need arises. This means that if you put $3000.00 dollars in your fund you defer $840.00 in Federal taxes @ 28 %. If you do well, and say you able to withdraw $5000.00 a month when you retire. You will pay $16,800.00 annually in Federal taxes. The Federal Government profits $15960.00 in the future. Plus you may have to pay your State taxes. Which will probably be higher. The 401k Roth savings plan and the Roth IRA don't allow the tax deduction up front, but you n**ever** pay State, Federal or Capital Gains taxes when you withdraw after age 59 ½ regardless of how much you make. So, in other words, if you don't need the tax deduction you would do better with a **401k Roth or Roth IRA**. You can make $20,000,000.00 draw on it monthly after retirement **TAX-FREE.** You can have as many IRA's as you like.

The choice is yours.

Let's say I do all my trading in a Roth IRA. Then I have a emergency need. I can draw cash from my Roth IRA. If it exceeds my principal, I only pay a 10% penalty on the gains portion. Which is considerably less than the 30% capital gains tax in a regular cash account. If I don't exceed the amount that I have contributed there is no penalty or tax.

You rollover your Traditional IRA to a Roth IRA [11]5 years before you approach retirement. They will take approximately 20%, but after that you won't have to pay taxes, State or Federal.

First time home buyers pay no penalty for withdrawing $10,000.00 to purchase a home even if it exceeds you contribution. For more information you can go to **MSN.COM**, click on **Investing,** then **Insights,** then **Planning** and in the top drop box click on **Retirement and Wills.** You will find valuable information there. If that's not enough type in **IRA** in the search engine slot. I am sure you will find a website that will have the information you seek.

Some 401k's allow you to trade your own personal selection of stocks inside your 401k. It's called **SELFDIRECTED** account. This is also capital gains tax free. Check with your mutual fund company to see if they offer self-directed accounts. Cigna Financial offers self- directed services. Your company Retirement board plan administrator must approve.Visit www.irs.gov. Type in IRA.

---

[11] The Roth must be open for 5 years before it gains tax exemption status.

# 401k Strategy

The easiest way to determine how much you will need to retire is to add a zero onto to your base pay and multiply it by 2. That will give you 20 years of income at that level. Just remember that the cost of living is definitely going to increase. Businesses are looking to either discontinue retirement plans or reduce their contribution.

The most common strategy for 401k's is to spread your money across three or four investments. They call this diversifying. This may be alright if you already have about $200,000.00. Diversifying with $500.00 in the beginning will result in slow growth. Plus every fund has cost associated with it and mutual fund companies have been reluctant to tell you about the 5 fees you have to pay. These fees will come from your investment, either at the beginning or at the end. The more funds you have the more fees you pay. That is money you won't get to invest.

Mutual funds are heavily diversified. They have as many as 150 to 1000 companies stocks listed. These companies cover the whole gambit of businesses, from medical to grocery to insurance and on. You name the business type, I guarantee you that your fund has it in there. This is another reasons for not having so many funds, sometimes 2 funds will have the same companies. [12]You don't need to buy the same companies from 2 different sources. You will be paying 2 sets of fees for the same stocks. You won't know this unless you read that all confusing **Prospectus** you throw away every year.

[12] How to make money in Stocks William J. O'neil pg. 236 paragraph 2

The investment industry alleges that your money is safe, if all your eggs aren't in one basket. This also limits how much money you make in a given amount of time, say 5 years. How many of you found out in 2000 that if you don't watch the baskets you will lose some eggs from a 401k mutual fund?

"If you put all your eggs in one basket, **watch the basket.**" One reason most people buy mutual funds is, because they think the broker is going to watch the basket. Not unless it has about $2,500,000.00 in it.

You will have to manage your retirement fund until you leave earth or get rich enough where you can pay some one to do it. I will say this mutual funds are easy to follow with charts and are less intense. They are excellent for someone who has made as much money as they feel they need. Charts will help them know when to move it to safety. Most of the funds are designed to follow one of the indexes such as the S&P 500 which can be followed on Bigcharts.com. If you click on the **Compare to** drop box at Bigcharts.com you will see a list of indexes. Find out from your financial institution which one it follows and track that index. You only need to do this if your fund doesn't have a stock symbol issued to it.

Mutual funds come in shares just like a stock. Some are traded just like a stock.

They have began to issue more of what are called Exchange Traded Funds (ETF). These are mutual funds that are traded intra-day like stocks. Normally mutual funds don't sell until the end of the day, regardless of when you place the order to sell. ETF's, trade just like a stock. What ever the price is at that time is what you buy or sell it for. Many companies today assign stock symbols to their funds today. Merrill Lynch and Franklin Templeton are good about issuing symbols. Newspapers list them. So you should approach mutual funds just like buying stocks. You should know when to buy and when to sell. You should know what you are buying. If you are just beginning you should focus on 1 fund. Yes I said it, [13]ONE FUND.

First find out the share price. Check out its performance for 1 year and 1 Quarter. They should both be positive. With the quarterly report you can allow a little latitude. Buy it until the share amount grows to 2500 shares. The time to accomplish this will determine on the amount of money you have. If possible view it on the chart. If it is still below the **support/resistance line** and the market is still in a growth mode add another 2500 shares. The market condition can be checked, by charting the NASDAQ and DOW. Use a 2 year/ weekly chart.

After that goal is reached, then you may want to look at another type of fund to begin building. Re-direct your contributions to the other fund. Don't transfer the money from the first fund to the new one. You can hold those 2500 or 5000 shares while you start a new objective. Now you're diversifying and making money at the same time.

The daily fluctuation of stock prices doesn't affect mutual funds much. I doubt that a mutual fund will grow $5.00 in one day let alone $10.00 like I have witnessed stocks do. If your fund is in the down phase, below the **Support/resistance line** or even beginning the upward move it doesn't matter. What matters is what the chart is showing you and what the market as a whole is showing. The market should be in a growth mode. If it isn't hold off buying stock funds until it is.

---

[13] How to make money in stocks, BY William O'neil pg.237 paragraph 3

If the fund starts to decline after a small climb of say $3.00 a share don't worry. You will be buying it cheaper on the way down. This is called Dollar cost averaging. You must however note the general direction of the market.

The goal here is that once you have accumulated the 2500 shares, if it is in a growth phase you will be earning $2500.00 everytime the fund goes up a dollar.

You have to use long range charts of at least 3 years in the **Time** frame. These are long term objectives. If the market is re-emerging after a recession or major decline like the one in 2000-2001 you will notice that the large cap funds don't do as well as small caps or mid caps in the beginning. Also if you are just beginning you should be buying small or mid cap funds. They have a longer time horizon. This will allow you more time to buy shares at a cheaper price. A mid cap company may have been a large cap before the recession. The decline in the stock price changed the cap status. So if they pick the right stocks, the mid cap will become a large cap. That's because the increase in stock price raises the market capitalization (**price of the outstanding shares multiplied times the share price**).

Let's say you have reached the maximum growth point. First what is the Chart showing? Second what is the Market doing? How long has it been since the last group of bankruptcies been filed by businesses? Count from 2002 add about 5 years and follow each group of 6 years. About 2006-2007 the bankruptcies will probably occur again resulting from a recession. If the market is doing well then that may not be the case. **Just keep your eye on the basket**.

The reason for observing market pattern is, that bankruptcies generally can only be filed every 7 years. These will be market decline years. Approximately 3 years out of the 7 will be down years or slow years. You will pick up the pattern.

When the market begins to decline that's when you want to look at moving every thing into some type of Guaranteed fund, Money market, Bond fund or something that grows with a guaranteed interest rate and is not as market sensitive. Some plans offer a investment vehicle for just that reason. During that down season you will be earning 3% or better on your money instead just letting it decline back to where it started. Declines can take up to 2 or more years to complete. The only way to know what is happening is by what the charts are showing you.

If your company doesn't provide a retirement fund and you have a 401k from a independent company, switch from the 401k to a Traditional IRA from Ameritrade. (Where I have mine) They allow you to buy both stocks and mutual funds at your discretion. Today Ford Motor Co. is trading a $6.90 a share. Ford is a tremendous investment at this price. Inside of a Roth IRA I can buy 1000 shares hold them until Ford reaches $30.00 or maybe even $40.00 a share and sell it **Tax Free.** No capital gains, no State or Federal Taxes ever. Even after I spend it in retirement at 59 1/2. The best thing is to look for another investment opportunity to multiply your gains. You don't want to marry a stock. Always look for a place to repeat the same growth.

# Biblical Principles on Investing

In this section I want to speak to my Christian brothers and sisters. I have been fortunate to witness Christianity to come out of the Dark ages in a number of areas, particularly where finance is concerned.

Look at Proverbs 13:22

**13:22 ¶ A good man leaveth an inheritance to his children's children: and the wealth of the sinner is laid up for the just. (KJV)**

Good men, should be striving to leave an inheritance large enough for their **Grandchildren.** Also with that, God has told you where the money is. The biggest pile of money I know of, that is laid up, is on Wall Street.

God want the sinners money so we can fund the Gospel and win the sinner. So they can get the sinners money to further the Gospel and win more sinners.

For whatever reason, some ministers still teach that Christians are supposed to be poor. They do this despite what Proverbs 13:22 says.

They also overlooked the fact, that it takes money to take the Gospel world wide, as we are commanded in Matthew 28:18,19. Plus the Bible authorized honorable Men of God to receive a salary from the gospel.

**I Cor. 9:11-14 If we have sown unto you spiritual things, is it a great thing if we shall reap your carnal things? crf. Ro 15:27; Ga 6:6**

**2 If others be partakers of this power over you, are not we rather?**

**Nevertheless we have not used this power; but suffer all things, lest we should hinder the gospel of Christ. crf. Ac 20:33; 1Co 9:15,18; 2Co 11:7,9; 12:13; 1Th 2:6; 2Co 11:12**

**13 Do ye not know that they which minister about holy things live of the things of the temple? and they which wait at the altar are partakers with the altar?**

**crf Le 6:16,26; 7:6; Nu 5:9,10; 18:8-20; De 10:9; 18:1**

**14 Even so hath the Lord ordained that they which preach the gospel should live of the gospel. crf. Mt 10:10; Lu 10:7; Ga 6:6; 1Ti 5:17**

Why would anyone want to deprive Men of God of substance? They deny their on personal agenda and pursuits. They strive to keep people from hell and lead them to heaven through the preaching of the Gospel.

They work hard. God doesn't expect them to live in poverty. In the Old Testament the priest were allowed to keep 10 % of the tithe to live off of. It seems to be normal thinking that if a person works they should be paid. We will pay teachers, and we will counselors, but we expect Men and Women of God to do it for free as though they don't sacrifice time and energy.

**Nu 18:24 But the tithes of the children of Israel, which they offer as an heave offering unto the LORD, I have given to the Levites to inherit: therefore I have said unto them, Among the children of Israel they shall have no inheritance.**

**25 And the LORD spake unto Moses, saying, 26 Thus speak unto the Levites, and say unto them, When ye take of the children of Israel the tithes which I have given you**

**from them for your inheritance, then ye shall offer up an heave offering of it for the LORD, even a tenth part of the tithe.**

**27 And this your heave offering shall be reckoned unto you, as though it were the corn of the threshingfloor, and as the fulness of the winepress.**

**28 Thus ye also shall offer an heave offering unto the LORD of all your tithes, which ye receive of the children of Israel; and ye shall give thereof the LORD'S heave offering to Aaron the priest.**

**29 Out of all your gifts ye shall offer every heave offering of the LORD, of all the best thereof, even the hallowed part thereof out of it.**

**(KJV)**

God will bless those who bless the Man or Woman of God. (hint, hint) Their main objective is to get the gospel out.

**Mt 28:18 And Jesus came and spake unto them, saying, All power is given unto me in heaven and in earth.**

**19 Go ye therefore, and teach all nations, baptizing them in the name of the Father, and of the Son, and of the Holy Ghost:**

Then there are the poor. God wants to use us to minister to them. To meet the needs of the poor **IT TAKES MONEY**. God has always expected us to prosper. It is His will for His Children. We can't feed the poor if we are broke.

Some people think that it is good to be broke as though it is some sign of humility. In reality they are only thinking about what they need and not the needs of others. Some even apply this false idealogy to their family. They, not God, allow their children to grow up in poverty and at the same time talk about how rich God is and how He loves His Children. Then their children look at unbelievers, and wonder what kind of God would neglect His own and take better care of sinners? No where in the Bible does God demand us to live in poverty. **There is no vow of poverty in the Bible.**

**3 John 2 Beloved, I wish above all things that thou mayest prosper and be in health, even as thy soul prospereth.**

**Joh 10:10 The thief cometh not, but for to steal, and to kill, and to destroy: I am come that they might have life, and that they might have it more abundantly.**

**Isaiah 48:17 The Lord who takes up your cause, the Holy One of Israel, says, I am the Lord your God, who is teaching you for your profit, guiding you by the way in which you are to go.**

These are just a few scriptures that let us know what God's will is concerning prosperity. I was once one of those that said "I don't want to be rich." I really didn't want to be, because being rich demands more responsibilty, which is probably why a lot of Christians avoid it. "What about what God needs?" You ask what does God need? **Glory, Recognition, Honor and Love**. He has a right to it. The reason God created man is to Glorify Him as a great God, not a broke God. We are His only means to operate in the earth. God gave control of earth to us. What do think **Dominion** means? Man is the primary reason for the poverty today. If you are one of those that say "I am rich in faith", prove it. Show some action. Try this for a simple definition of faith. **F**ervent **A**ction **I**n **T**rusting **H**im.

Let's look at what James say's about this issue.

**James 2:14-20**

**14 What doth it profit, my brethren, though a man say he hath faith, and have not works? can faith save him?**

**15 If a brother or sister be naked, and destitute of daily food,**

**16 And one of you say unto them, Depart in ye give them not those things which are needful to the body; what doth it profit?**

**17 Even so faith, if it hath not works, is dead, being alone.**

**18 Yea, a man may say, Thou hast faith, and I have works: shew me thy faith without thy works, and I will shew thee my faith by my works.**

**19 Thou believest that there is one God; thou doest well: the devils also believe, and tremble.**

**20 But wilt thou know, O vain man, that FAITH WITHOUT WORKS IS DEAD?**

The reason God gives us faith, is so we can accomplish His will. Some of you want to wait until you get to heaven to have riches. You should consider that if you don't know what your responsibility to God is concerning riches, you **may** wind up not fulfilling **the will of God** for your life. Thereby, disobeying God, you wind up barely making it into heaven and have no reward waiting. One other thing, what good would wealth do in a place where everything is free? You do know that in heaven everything is paid for?

Let's begin with stewardship. This is where most of problems lie. You must realize that your money **isn't really your money.** In case you forgot everything belongs to God. We are only managers. If you think I'm wrong, note how many people take it with them when they die. I wonder what they present to God?

Anyway, look at Matthew 25:14-30

**14 For the kingdom of heaven is as a man travelling into a far country, who called his own servants, and delivered unto them his goods. 15 And unto one he gave five talents, to another two, and to another one; to every man according to his several ability; and straightway took his journey. {talents: a talent is one hundred and eighty seven pounds ten shillings}**

**16 Then he that had received the five talents went and traded with the same, and made them other five talents.**

**17 And likewise he that had received two, he also gained other two.**

**18 But he that had received one went and digged in the earth, and hid his lord's money.**

**19 After a long time the lord of those servants cometh, and reckoneth with them.**

**20 And so he that had received five talents came and brought other five talents, saying, Lord, thou deliveredst unto me five talents: behold, I have gained beside them five talents more.**

**21 His lord said unto him, Well done, thou good and faithful servant: thou hast been faithful over a few things, I will make thee ruler over many things: enter thou into the joy of thy lord.**

**22 He also that had received two talents came and said, Lord, thou deliveredst unto me two talents: behold, I have gained two other talents beside them.**

**23 His lord said unto him, Well done, good and faithful servant; thou hast been faithful over a few things, I will make thee ruler over many things: enter thou into the joy of thy lord.**

**24 Then he which had received the one talent came and said, Lord, I knew thee that thou art an hard man, reaping where thou hast not sown, and gathering where thou hast not strawed:**

**25 And I was afraid, and went and hid thy talent in the earth: lo, there thou hast that is thine.**

**26 His lord answered and said unto him, Thou wicked and slothful servant, thou knewest that I reap where I sowed not, and gather where I have not strawed**

**27 Thou oughtest therefore to have put my money to the exchangers (bank), and then at my coming I should have received mine own with usury( interest).**

**28 Take therefore the talent from him, and give it unto him which hath ten talents.**

**29 For unto every one that hath shall be given, and he shall have abundance: but from him that hath not shall be taken away even that which he hath.**

**30 And cast ye the unprofitable servant into outer darkness: there shall be weeping and gnashing of teeth.**

This scripture is primarily about adding souls to the kingdom of God. Notice that money is a primary tool for service. Nothing is more important to God than saved souls. God expects us to multiply what He gives us, so he can do what needs to be done in the earth.

Notice, the first servant had 5 talents. For the sake of argument let's say it was $5.00. Back then it was equivalent to

$5000.00 today. Notice that he **Traded** and in some translations he "put the money to work".

Simply put, he invested it. The one with the 2 talents did the same. Remember earlier when I talked about the 100 % trade method? Now you know where I got it from. You thought I invented it didn't you? Nottttttt.

Notice also that the rich got richer off of the one who didn't observe how to invest. If you lost money in the market guess who got it? The Short traders and Put buyers.

There are different types of investing methods. The principle is to get more than you originally started out with.

Starting a business, buying, selling or renting out real estate is investing. Getting an education to increase your income is investing. Know this beloved, God has given you something to work with. It is up to you to find out from Him what it is.

Do you believe God can make an Investor/ Business person out of you? Regardless of your education or the lack of it? God can, with your cooperation, get you to the place of prosperity He desires for you to be. Then you can be a financial benefit to work of the Gospel of Jesus Christ. Notice in these next verses that God gave His super these men natural ability.

**Exodus 31:1-6**

**1 And the LORD spake unto Moses, saying,**

**2 See, I have called by name Bezaleel the son of Uri, the son of Hur, of the tribe of Judah:**

**3 And I have filled him with the spirit of God, in wisdom, and in understanding, and in knowledge, and in all manner of workmanship,**

**4 To devise cunning works, to work in gold, and in silver, and in brass,**

**5 And in cutting of stones, to set them, and in carving of timber, to work in all manner of workmanship.**

**6 And I, behold, I have given with him Aholiab, the son of Ahisamach, of the tribe of Dan: and in the hearts of all that are wise hearted I have put wisdom, that they may make all that I have commanded thee;**

Notice, God gave His Superpower to the natural ability to Bezaleel and Aholiab to help accomplish the task He gave Moses. Your Pastor has a task. God has by way of the Holy Spirit gave His superpower to your natural ability. This is to help you help your Pastor carry out the task that God has given him.

**John 14: 26 But the Comforter, which is the Holy Ghost, whom the Father will send in my name, he shall teach you ALL things, and bring all things to your remembrance, whatsoever I have said unto you.**

Let's look at a situation, where cooperation with God, helped a woman who had no experience at all start a oil business.

**2 Kings 4:1-7**

**1 Now there cried a certain woman of the wives of the sons of the prophets unto Elisha, saying, Thy servant my husband is dead; and thou knowest that thy servant did fear the LORD: and the creditor is come to take unto him my two**

**sons to be bondmen.**

**2 And Elisha said unto her, What shall I do for thee? tell me, what hast thou in the house? And she said, Thine handmaid hath not any thing in the house, save a pot of oil.**

**3 Then he said, Go, borrow thee vessels abroad of all thy neighbours, even empty vessels; borrow not a few.**

**4 And when thou art come in, thou shalt shut the door upon thee and upon thy sons, and shalt pour out into all those vessels, and thou shalt set aside that which is full.**

**5 So she went from him, and shut the door upon her and upon her sons, who brought the vessels to her; and she poured out.**

**6 And it came to pass, when the vessels were full, that she said unto her son, Bring me yet a vessel. And he said unto her, There is not a vessel more. And the oil stayed.**

**7 Then she came and told the man of God. And he said, Go, sell the oil, and pay thy debt, and live thou and thy children of the rest.**

Now this woman could have easily said "I don't know how to sell oil." or "I don't want to get into the oil selling business." Instead, she did what the Man of God instructed. You have the Holy Spirit. He knows what you need to do to get to A, and from A to B and from B to C. God has given you a ***Anointing*** ([14] The burden removing, yoke destroying power of God, [15]that comes by the Love of God, to accomplish the Will God). The Anointing works because God loves you. He has given it to you to get His will for you done. But I am absolutely, totally convinced, He has made a way for you. It is up to you, to find out from Him, what to do.

If your Pastor doesn't have a vision for soul winning and the development of the Body of Christ, you really should to pray about that. The time for dead, do nothing churches, is long past. They should be buried with everything else that is dead.

---

[14] Authors translation

[15] Author's definition of Anointing

I believe God wants His own schools and universities, where there will be no debate about the posting of the Ten Commandments or Pictures of Jesus Christ. Where creation is taught, instead of the frequently changing, un-provable, atheistic **theory** of **evilution**. They know that a tadpole can't turn into a fish, to a ape, to a man. There is no D.N.A. match possible to establish that foolishness.

It takes more faith to believe that, than "In the beginning God". We can have everything that the world has and better. We can and should set the standard for business. But it takes money. I am not suggesting that we separate ourselves into a commune. That would defeat the purpose of the Gospel. But I believe we can have a designer line of clothing better than what they have. We have God to give us revelation they can't even imagine.

We can open our own hospitals and research facilities. There the nurses and doctors can pray before and after surgery. Lay hands on the patients for their quick recovery. I believe God will give us revelation for cures of all the major diseases.

# The debt/devourer system

Now a little bit about this debt monster. Do the G.O.O.D. thang, **Get Out Of Debt.** Debt is not a blessing. Look at the difference between these verses of scripture found in Deuteronomy chapter 28. Verses 1-12 are promises of blessing which are ours because of Jesus Christ (Galatians 3:29) and 28:15 & 44 are curses for not consulting with God about finances.

**Deut. 28:1, 12**

**28:1 And it shall come to pass, if thou shalt hearken/ listen diligently unto the voice of the LORD thy God, to observe and to do all his commandments which I command thee this day, that the LORD thy God will set thee on high above**

**all nations of the earth:**

**28: 12 The LORD shall open unto thee his good treasure, the heaven to give the rain unto thy land in his season, and to bless all the work of thy hands. thou shalt lend unto many nations, and thou shalt not borrow.**

Notice in verse 12. He said we would lend unto many nations and shall not borrow. He didn't say you couldn't borrow. But you should know that a blessing is a **asset** and not a **liability.** The key is listening to the **Voice of the Lord.**

**YOU** will have to become personal with God, not your Pastor, deacon, minister, church lady, it must be **YOU** and God. In other words **YOU** will have to learn to pray. You will have to spend time in the presence of God. You might want to get a copy

**Prayers that avail much by Word ministries**

available at most Christian book stores. If not, the

**ISBN no. is 0-89274-950-4**.

God loves to talk with His children. You can be confident He will direct you in what to do. Now look at the curse portion and particularly verses 15 and 44.

**28:15 But it shall come to pass, if you will not hearken/ listen unto the voice of the LORD thy God, to observe to do all his commandments and**

**his statutes which I command thee this day; that all these curses shall come upon thee, and overtake thee:**

**28:43 The stranger that is within thee shall get up above thee very high; and thou shalt come down very low.**

**44 He shall lend to thee, and thou shalt not lend to him: he shall be the head, and thou shalt be the tail.**

You can choose whether to operate under the curse/liability by not listening to God or blessing/asset . Remember God isn't obligated to help you pay off debt you chose to get into. He does it because He knew we were ignorant of His word for generations. You can see the grace period for this issue is ending. Even the world is saying get out of debt. A Blessing is a asset and a asset is profit/ gain. Credit beyond your ability to pay in 30 days is pure unadulterated liability /loss. The new debit cards are the real way that credit cards were intended to be used. But Visa saw a golden goose and they are pumping golden eggs out every second. They will let you have a credit card that is half your income.

God loves you and He isn't double minded. He knows how this system works. Servitude is not His intention for His children. Debt is servitude.

**Proverb 22: 7 ¶ The rich ruleth over the poor, and the borrower is servant to the lender.**

So if you have been under the delusion that having high debt, that consumes your income and prevents you from saving and investing is a good thing, think about what these scriptures are saying.

I know you are probably saying how can I buy a house if I don't get in debt? Well try this. First start paying your way out of debt. Give your self about 2 years to save up some money. Check with the local county or state office about aquiring property that is disposed of for overdue taxes. Check the legal newspaper if there is one near. In there you see what properties facing foreclosure. Learn how the system works. Find out if someone in your church is a Probate attorney or if anyone knows of a good one. Go to the auction even if you aren't ready to buy at this time. Observe the rules and actions of the buyers. I bought my first property for 5% of it's value. The restoration cost less than 10%, giving me 85% equity. You may be able to mortgage property for 70% of the equity then sell the house. If I am right you don't have to pay taxes on borrowed money**. Check with a local tax consultant. Be prayerful** so Holy Spirit can educate you as you watch. You may even want start a group of real estate investors. This will make it easier if your capital is low. **Psalm 105:42-44**

Start looking for someone who does home repair such as plumbing, electrical, carpentry etc. Get organized, as you do Holy Spirit will guide you. God believes in preparation.

It may be unlikely that you will find the house you want to live in. You will find some that can be sold. Buy a copy of Home buying for Dummies or something close to that. It will help you avoid property pitfalls. **Above all pray before you buy.** Only God knows what you can't see. **Make sure the center of your**

**being (not your head, yo gut) is at peace**. Buy and sell until you get the home that you want **Debt Free**. Obviously you will continue to buy until you are a Trillionaire. (smile).

You may want to look into buying foreclosed property, after you have accumulated some capital.

You may find what you are looking for there. You may want to purchase as a group, the Carleton Sheets program. He provides a lot of information that is very useful. When buying or bidding don't go past 50% equity. The idea is to make money, not just own profitless property.

If you have some equity in your property, that is enough for you to buy foreclosed or probated property, then use it. But as soon as you can, put it back. Again **Pray** before taking the equity out, **God knows the time.**

Another means for making money are Flea markets and garage sales. You can get items to sell at a garage sale from your local storage facility. Call them and ask them when they will be auctioning off property left in storage. They sell the property when renters neglect to pay their rental fee.

Go and watch the auctions. Plan how you will store what you buy. You get the whole bin when you win the bid. I bought a whole 10 ft wide bin for $50.00. I had beds and TV's all over the place. Watch for valuable artifacts also. You'd be surprised what people leave behind. Some items may even be sold through Ebay or other online auction sites. Some of this stuff got left behind due to death of the owner. What you don't sell donate to the locate charity for fair market value. If you file 1040 income taxes you can use the receipts for tax deduction.

For the auto mechanically inclined, find the local auto auction. If you go online to Kelly Bluebook.com or KBB.COM, you will find the market value for the car. Under sell the market in your area. Don't try for maximum profit. Go for about $500.00 a sale. Lawn service and home cleaning service are big these days. Ladies you can run a lawn service as a manager and hire some young men to do the work while you manage the money and quality control. Men you can do the same thing with cleaning service. Some of you probably have been given management skill you've never used. You can never tell what you will find out if you pray.

Lastly, World Business exchange Network at WWW.WBE.NET is for those who want to work from home with a computer. They help you find overseas businesses that have product needs. You find the product through the internet or newspaper. You connect the product with the business and get a commission.

**Ps 105:42 For he remembered his holy promise, and Abraham his servant.**
**43 And he brought forth his people with joy, and his chosen with gladness:**
**44 And gave them the lands of the heathen: and they inherited the labour of the people; (KJV)**

# Tithes and Offering

Too many Christians take **Tithe** (the tenth) paying and giving an offering to lightly. This is one of the single most important key's to financial victory. Plus, have you considered what the penalty is for consistent robbery? Look at Malachi 3:8-12.

**Mal. 3:8 Will a man keep back from God what is right? But you have kept back what is mine.**

**But you say, What have we kept back from you? Tithes and offerings.**

**9 You are cursed with a curse; for you have kept back from me what is mine, even all this nation.**

**10 Let your tithes come into the store-house so that there may be food in my house, and put me to the test (confirm the truth of my word) by doing so, says the Lord of armies, and see if I do not make the windows open (allow the flow)**

**of heaven (light, illumination, revelation knowledge of ideas, whitty inventions and business opportunities) and send down such a blessing (power to prosper) on you that there is no room (capacity to receive it all at once, so it will continue for generations) for it.**

**11 And on your account I will keep back the locusts (Devourer) from wasting the fruits of your land; and the fruit of your vine will not be dropped on the field before its time (I will maintain and protect what I have given you), says the Lord of armies.**

**12 And you will be named happy by all nations: for you will be a land of delight, says the Lord of armies.**

For those that say that was the Old testament let's look at what Jesus does with your tithes when you pay them.

**Hebrew 7: 8 And here men that die receive tithes; but there He (Jesus) receiveth them, of whom it is witnessed that He (Jesus) liveth.**

Do you believe that Jesus is alive? Is He your High Priest? Do you think God lied? Can God be trusted? Then what is your reason for not paying your tithes? Afraid your credit will go bad? Which would you rather have? Good credit or right standing with God and the blessings of God? Do you really think He will let you fail? God isn't testing you, He's say's TEST HIM. He said prove Him, test the integrity of His Word. He say's He, not your Pastor will open up the windows of heaven.

Listen beloved, God isn't trying take something from you, He's trying to get something to you. Tithes belong to Him. He really has no obligation to give you back anything. He is trying to get you to be like Him. He wants you to give solely for the benefit of others. He wants giving motivated by love and not need.

When you give, He can maintain a place where others can get saved, and learn how to stay saved by being taught the word. If need be they can come to His house to get food and clothing. If you demonstrate that He can depend on you, to allow money to flow through you, He will make sure it get's to you.

If you spend time in prayer and meditation He will reveal what steps you can take to become very prosperous.

## Protecting your investments

I can't give you all the details. I would have to be an Tax Attorney. But I can point you in the right direction. There is a system called **Limited Liability Partnerships or corporations,(LLP and LLC) Living Trust and Charitable remainder trust**. This is the best way to operate a investment club or group.

Basically this system which is used by the rich and the wise. It is designed to lower your taxes, protect your assets from lawsuits and help you main tain the wealth you accumulate.

Go to **http://me.investortoolbox.com/products/taxplanning.html** call the hotline and ask when the next seminar is going to be in your area. You may even want to drive a couple of hundred miles to this. Ask for some complimentary tickets. It will be worth the trip.

You may want to use their service or you may not, but you will know exactly what to do. I doubt that any other attorney will beat their price, plus give you the support you may need.

If you have rental property or plan to, this information is absolutely necessary. Remember with property you are only one lawsuit away from disaster. With this protection if you are sued and they win they can **never** collect, but they will get a tax bill from the I.R.S. for winnings they can never possess. This is the age when people are suing churches, so you know you better protect yourself. Also the Charitable remainder trust will allow you to transfer the wealth to your children without them having to pay estate taxes or go to probate court in the event your death. You will be able to maintain control of your wealth as long as you are on earth. **Go to the seminar**.

Well I hoped I have peeked your interest in Internet

investing. May God bless your every endeavor.

Pick up a copy of:

Online Investing by Jon Markman

ISBN 0-7356-0650-1

Online Investing for Dummies

ISBN 0-7645-0725-7.

God's Plan for your finances by Dwight Nichols

ISBN 088-368-5094.

**Jim Cramer's Real Money: Sane Investing in an Insane World.**

**All Available through any online bookstore.**

**How to make money in stocks**

**William J. Oneil**

**ISBN 007140668**

They will be of great service and a worth while investment. You absolutely **must buy** a copy of **Robbing you Blind by Mark Dempsey ISBN 0-688-**

**17034-X**. This book will tell you all the fallacies about mutual funds, brokers, financial advisors, and even the S.E.C. and how they work against you.

# About the Author

Like most Americans, Richard was oblivious to how a 401k operated. One day he spoke to a financial advisor. He was shocked to discover that the money that he saved in his 401k was all he would have to live from.

Shortly after the same financial advisor quit their job to become a Day trader. She began to show him a better way to invest. After seeing 200% increase in a investment in 31 days he began research how the stock market worked. In doing so he discovered that the Internet gave him education, research and control over his stock choices. Gleaning information from many resources he has developed a simple understandable guide to help the less than average investor stop losing their investments.

You can contact him at Investorhelp@comcast.net

www.ingramcontent.com/pod-product-compliance
Ingram Content Group UK Ltd.
Pitfield, Milton Keynes, MK11 3LW, UK
UKHW041929190726
13854UKWH00004B/1527

9 781410 796592